Love and Death in
Edith Wharton's Fiction

**MODERN
AMERICAN
LITERATURE**
New Approaches

Yoshinobu Hakutani
General Editor

Vol. 48

PETER LANG
New York • Washington, D.C./Baltimore • Bern
Frankfurt am Main • Berlin • Brussels • Vienna • Oxford

Tricia M. Farwell

Love and Death in Edith Wharton's Fiction

PETER LANG
New York • Washington, D.C./Baltimore • Bern
Frankfurt am Main • Berlin • Brussels • Vienna • Oxford

Library of Congress Cataloging-in-Publication Data
Farwell, Tricia M.
Love and death in Edith Wharton's fiction / Tricia M. Farwell.
p. cm. — (Modern American literature: new approaches; v. 48)
Includes bibliographical references and index.
1. Wharton, Edith, 1862–1937—Criticism and interpretation.
2. Spiritual life in literature. 3. Death in literature.
4. Love in literature. I. Title. II. Series: Modern
American literature (New York, N.Y.); v. 48.
PS3545.H16Z6465   813'.52—dc22   2005017859
ISBN 0-8204-7943-8
ISSN 1078-0521

Bibliographic information published by **Die Deutsche Bibliothek**.
Die Deutsche Bibliothek lists this publication in the "Deutsche
Nationalbibliografie"; detailed bibliographic data is available
on the Internet at http://dnb.ddb.de/.

The paper in this book meets the guidelines for permanence and durability
of the Committee on Production Guidelines for Book Longevity
of the Council of Library Resources.

© 2006 Peter Lang Publishing, Inc., New York
29 Broadway, New York, NY 10006
www.peterlang.com

All rights reserved.
Reprint or reproduction, even partially, in all forms such as microfilm,
xerography, microfiche, microcard, and offset strictly prohibited.

Printed in Germany

For my parents, Knight and Nancy Farwell

Contents

Chapter One
Introduction — 1

Chapter Two
"The Fullness of Life" — 13

Chapter Three
The House of Mirth — 23

Chapter Four
The Fruit of the Tree — 45

Chapter Five
Ethan Frome — 65

Chapter Six
The Reef — 79

Chapter Seven
Summer — 95

Chapter Eight
The Glimpses of the Moon — 107

Chapter Nine
Twilight Sleep — 123

Chapter Ten
The Buccaneers — 135

Chapter Eleven
Conclusion — 149

Bibliography	153
Index	159

CHAPTER ONE

Introduction

It seems that the greatest romances always link love and death. In many of these, the lovers' deaths serve to prove that their love will endure into the afterlife, for all eternity. Although the ability of love to survive in life and through all eternity is often seen as the ideal, Edith Wharton uses the connection between love and death throughout her works to discover what a true ideal love match really is.

Wharton's struggle with differing notions of love reveals itself by examining the connection between love and death, Eros and Thanatos, in her works. Love, as depicted throughout her writings, is more than just a reenactment of her unhappy marriage and subsequent affair. Instead, the role of Thanatos in romantic relationships serves to highlight the central conflict Wharton saw as implicit in the concept of love, the struggle between desiring a spiritual, "platonic," love and a physical, erotic, love. Both forms of love have their roots in prominent philosophic and scientific works that Wharton read by Plato, Charles Darwin, and Sigmund Freud. Throughout her writing, Wharton portrayed love as a struggle between the romantic notion of soul mates finding each other and the realistic view of sexual selection. However, actually coming to a solid conclusion about what constitutes true love was not an easy task. It was truly only with her final work that Wharton eventually came to terms with both forms of love to depict a potentially happy union where characters were able to balance the two extremes.

The prominence of love in Wharton's works has not gone unnoticed by Wharton scholars. However, the majority of the criticism relates to her writing her real-life unhappy marriage and subsequent affair, and her characters' disillusionment with love and marriage. In this view, when Wharton was "trapped" in an unhappy marriage, she wrote dejected romances. When Wharton had her sexual awakening via an affair with

Morton Fullerton, the passion she felt for him emerged in her writing (Lewis; Erlich; Wolff, *Feast*). Although Wharton may not have been totally fulfilled in her marriage, she "was herself a romantic, who could not abandon the belief that there was a perfect soulmate [sic] for most people, even if there was not one for her" (Goodman, *Women*, 104). In her fiction, much as in her life, the path to finding and keeping one's soul mate was never easy. However, there is more to her romances than her personal quest for her soul mate and a depiction of Wharton's personal frustrations with her marriage.

Despite the attention Wharton's works are currently receiving, few studies focus primarily on love in relation to Wharton's interest in science and philosophy. The studies which do examine her use of the erotic tend to focus on her gothic works or ghost stories. These scholars chose to focus on the ghost stories and gothic elements because the genres allowed Wharton greater freedom in the depiction of women's erotic nature.

Others have noticed that marriage is rarely a positive element in her fiction. Wai-chee Dimock argues that female characters use sex to gain power in the marriage market. In doing this, relationships become business transactions, not love matches. Essentially, love is removed from socially successful relationships when they are beneficial monetary matches. Flirtation does not fare well in Wharton's world either. Richard Kaye, in his examination of the role of flirtation in relationships, argued that it allowed male characters to delay their erotic desires, sometimes to the point of the female character's death. This inability to commit to their loves is part of the reason so many of Wharton's male characters are lacking (Holbrook).

Perhaps scholars have found discussing Wharton's depictions of romantic relationships unsettling because the relationships portrayed have more in common with sentimental novels than the realist tradition commonly associated with the author. Hildegard Hoeller argued that Wharton's use of elements of both realist fiction and sentimental fiction allowed Wharton to depict her characters' full lives. Throughout her analysis, Hoeller hoped to force scholars to "reconsider" realistic and sentimental fictions thus removing some of the stigma associated with sentimental fiction (x).

Despite the relatively bleak nature of most of Wharton's works, and the significant amount of death surrounding her characters, the role of death in her fiction has not received much attention from scholars. When death is discussed, it is most often to question whether Lily Bart's suicide was intentional and to examine how staged it was. As an example, Cynthia

Griffin Wolff argues that Lily Bart's death is the ultimate theatrical ending to Lily's struggle for selfhood ("Lily").

Taking their lead from Wharton's letters, current trends in Wharton criticism are engaging in her dialogues with philosophy and science (Bender, Singley). In spite of Bender's and Singley's works, scholars have not fully examined the effect of science and philosophy upon Wharton's depictions of romance. In the following pages, I will argue that Wharton's lifelong interest in Darwin's writing was in direct conflict with the philosophical ideals expressed in Plato's dialogues, in which she was also interested at the time of writing several novels. The tension found between Darwin's version of a physical love and Plato's version of a spiritual love is the main tension throughout Wharton's life and works until she was able to allow her characters to find an ideal love in life.

As R. W. B. Lewis mentions in his discussion of Wharton's poem "The Last Giustiniani," Wharton often juxtaposed these two types of love against each other. This struggle of the "sacred as against earthly love was a theme" which she would continue to discuss in subsequent works (*Biography* 60). Wharton does, indeed, revisit this theme. In fact, she never leaves it. Instead, she refined her philosophy on spiritual love and earthly (physical) love throughout her fiction. Her philosophy of love becomes clearer when one looks at the interaction between Eros and spiritual love under the shadow of Thanatos. In Wharton's fictional world, her philosophy of love moves from the belief that death (Thanatos) makes love available only beyond the earthly realm to a belief that the ability to see beyond the earthly allows for a sensitive soul to awaken to its soul mate.

Wharton's interest in spiritual love being in conflict with physical love may have been influenced by her reading. Although it is well known that Wharton was interested in scientific theory of the time, she was also acquainted with Plato's *Dialogues*, especially the *Phaedrus* and the *Symposium*. From a letter written to Sarah Norton, we know that she was reading the *Symposium* as early as 1906 (Lewis and Lewis, 106). She may have read it even earlier than that, since according to Ramsden's catalog of Wharton's library, she possessed an 1875 edition of Plato's *Dialogues*.

The foundation of Plato's philosophy is the notion that there is an ideal form for each concept. He built this belief on the division of the body and the soul. When the human soul glimpses the ideal before entering a physical body, that ideal remained with the soul which allows humans to be able to generalize terms once they have learned the word for the ideal. For example, a person knows love because the soul has seen an ideal form of "love-ness." Therefore, a human knows than "love" can apply to an erotic love or a more spiritual love, even though the types of love do not have exactly the same characteristics. The *Symposium* is Plato's dialogue focusing on the nature and desire to understand love. These discussions defined and elucidated the tension between Eros, or sexual desire, and Platonic love, or soul love. While physical procreation may be love's expression of desire, mental procreation is love's long-term goal of beauty through goodness and wisdom. In seeking love, a soul seeks wisdom of the philosophers and, in essence, a greater connection for immortality. In terms of love, mental procreation is more beautiful than physical. While sex, or physical love, is not the ultimate end, the soul's reaching a complete union with the ideal beautiful soul is. Yet, if Eros is not controlled, it can become one's complete focus, thus keeping the soul from reaching the ideal union it desires by maintaining focus on the physical elements of love. However, both types of love share one common element: the desire to be completely united with another for "immortality" and "goodness" (Plato, *Symposium* 49).

In an attempt to define love and lovers, the *Phaedrus* also tackles the interaction between Eros and the soul's desire to reach the ideal union. The soul, according to Socrates' speech, is self-motion which causes the soul to seek the beautiful and good. In fact, "when it [the soul] is perfect and fully winged, it soars...if it loses its wings,...it can fasten on something solid" (*Phaedrus* 28). Fastening on to the physical keeps the soul from its flight to the beautiful union it seeks. Therefore, the soul must keep in motion in order to reach the gods and beauty. Unfortunately, the body keeps the soul trapped, unable to soar; it is a binding physical force (*Phaedrus* 34). Only when the soul reunites with the beautiful ideal can happiness be achieved. Sex, in the form of lust, works against the soul's desire and keeps it from finding happiness through love. Plato's establishing the primacy of the soul over the physical erotic places him in direct opposition to Darwin, whom Wharton openly described as being "one of the formative influences" upon her (Lewis and Lewis, 136).

Darwin's theory of sexual selection removes the romance of the soul from the concept of love and replaces it with a purely physical drive for procreation. There is no flying of the soul to meet with a greater beauty. Lovers obtain immortality through their offspring, not though the wisdom and beauty of the good. For Darwin, love was just one of the "social instincts" that move people to act to perpetuate the species (*Descent* 2:391). Love, itself a product of evolution to encourage procreation, was put to service of the physical. In order for the species to survive, a potential mate selected its partner through the process of sexual selection. The best mates were selected based on a variety of physical traits seen to be most beneficial to the survival of the species. The best were the best because their forefathers had cultivated these traits in order to make their offspring better, stronger and more viable. The selection of a mate was a competition where the best would fight to be selected by the best. It is a woman's external beauty, along with class standing, which becomes essential for men in the selection of a mate. Women, according to Darwin, sought money, power and physical strength as the key elements in their mates. By basing his theory of love on competition and physical beauty, Darwin emphasizes the physicality of relationships. Sex, or physical "love," is the foundation upon which he built his theory. The soul, in essence, has no real function in love as described by Darwin. Whereas Plato found the soul to be king of love, Darwin found the physical nature of sex to be dominant. Wharton, as we will see shortly, found this dichotomy problematic. It is even stated explicitly in her early short story, "The Fullness of Life."

As Bert Bender proved in his book *The Descent of Love*, Darwin's theory exerted a strong influence on the way authors viewed romance. Concepts governing sexual selection appeared frequently in courtship literature, and Wharton was "a transitional figure" in the dialogue (314). In addition, Wharton was "quite consciously engaged in the long-term study and controversy over modern love that developed" (322). Key to this analysis is that Wharton was conscious of what she was doing in using Darwinian Theory in her works. It was not accidental that so many of his ideas appeared in her depiction of courtship. She granted that female choice governed the selection of mates but that choice often led to imprisonment (325). Thus, she found at least part of his theory inadequate. She needed something more to complete her ideal notion of love.

Along with Plato and Darwin, Wharton was acquainted with Freud's inroads into explaining human behavior through the conscious and unconscious motives governing humanity. Through his studies, Freud not only provided a language for psychoanalytic theory, but also analyzed the motivations governing human behavior. As part of his research, he articulated that the battle between Eros and Thanatos was an essential battle taking place within an individual's psyche. Freud found that "these two instincts were struggling with each other from the very first" (*Beyond* 73). The struggle between these instincts is what governs all humans. In *Beyond the Pleasure Principle*, he brought Thanatos to the forefront in describing human desires. This death wish, or death instinct, is as much a part of human life as is the instinct for life. Thus, inside of everyone is a constant tension between the desire for life and the desire for death. The struggle is often an aggressive fight until the unconscious can bring the two instincts into balance. Eros, the life instinct, worked to assimilate the individual into the family and, by association, into civilization.

Yet, humans are not simple creatures. The unconscious force working against Eros, Thanatos, also works to preserve the individual self as part of the ego (*Beyond* 63). Conflict arises when one realizes that while Eros is striving for life, Thanatos is striving for death within the mind and body of each individual. Despite this tension, these two instincts always appear together. Thanatos "could be pressed into the service of Eros, in that the organism was destroying some other thing, whether animate or inanimate, instead of destroying its own self" (Freud, *Civilization* 78). When Thanatos expresses itself as Eros, "the erotic aim" is "twisted" into sadism or masochism (*Civilization* 81). The battle rages on inside the individual until the unconscious brings Eros and Thanatos into balance. This battle is at the core of every person. As a 1922 letter to Bernard Berenson testifies, Wharton was familiar with "Freudianism & all its jargon" (Lewis and Lewis, 451). In this letter, she warns one friend to deter another friend from reading Freud's work in order for that person "to develop the conscious" before "taking like a duck to—sewage" to the notions of the unconscious (451).

Building on the Freudian notion of the unconscious, Lacan claimed that there is a strong structural parallel between language and the unconscious. In the role of discourse, the unconscious becomes the subject's "history" (52). Because of this, the psychoanalyst should study the function of the speech of his patient. In addition to linking speech with the unconscious, Lacan also found that the transformation of a subject to an image which takes place in the mirror stage to be the entering of the subject into the symbolic order. Once the subject becomes an image, the subject begins to formulate a desire for the other (5). The only way to break free of the symbolic order is to "find the permanence of the concept," thus moving away from the "absence" inherent in words (65). According to Lacan, Freud's use of the *Fort! Da!* game exemplifies how the subject equates absence with desire and desire with absence. The concept of desire as absence also appears in death. Death "essentially express[es] the limit of the historical function" of a person thus ending the creative part of the person's life story (Lacan 103). In this way, the person becomes a fixed concept and "this death constitutes in the subject an eternalization of his desire" (104). Desire is eternal in death because death marks an eternal absence from the symbolic order. The subject is moved from all historicity and human's life is defined by human's history.

In his interpretation of Freud's theory, Brown takes the interaction of history and desire one step further, claiming that desire, not reason, rules history. Thus, love is the ruling concept of history and life. The tension between the instincts of life and death becomes the tension between "love and hate, love and aggression, love and the will to power" (53). Yet, these desires are founded upon a purely pleasurable conception of sexuality established in childhood. In art the ego, also known as the death instinct, is dominant (Brown 56). It is through art, however, that the unconscious becomes conscious. It sheds light on drives and instincts that the conscious self normally keeps repressed and under complete control. In this way, art becomes a vehicle to undo repressed and unconscious instincts. Because the death instinct is to create a beneficial life for the individual self and the life instinct is to bring the individual into the group, to repress death would be to repress oneself. In the end, in the tension between Eros and Thanatos, Eros enhances Thanatos, just as Thanatos enhances Eros.

With science and philosophy working so hard to define and describe the conflict between love and death, it is not surprising to find a similar tension enacted in literature. Death has always been prominent in the humanities for decades. In fact, one of the "hallmark[s]" of Victorian literature was the "inability to explore sex without concurrently exploring mortality" (Barreca 3). This connection reinforces the notion that sex and death enhance and explain each other. Often the main concern of death in the humanities was the expression of the meaning and effect of death for the living (Scholl 13). The author could depict death as ranging from a beautiful thing to merely a fact of life.

Many of the most prominent depictions of death are in connection with women. One of the most common representations of the dead woman is to inspire the men around her to greater achievements (Bronfen, "Dialogue"

242). The inspiration comes from the fact "that death transforms the body of a woman into the source of poetic inspiration precisely because it creates and gives corporality to a loss or absence" (Bronfen, "Dialogue" 242–3). With the woman becoming a physical representation of absence, the memory of her while alive becomes an open space for creation. Her lacking a body, a life, makes it impossible for her to rewrite whatever image a man elects to create for her, thus turning her into a source of creative inspiration. She not only becomes a site for his creating her story, but also a site for his creating his story, making a name for himself regarding her.

The ultimate expression of women, sex and death became the credo of the Victorian age, through the concept of the angel in the house. This view of the woman denies her an independent identity outside of the realm of Eros while expecting her to remain ignorant of sex. She was to marry and procreate within the bounds of marriage, but enjoy nothing and remain deceptively ignorant about the process. She was to be a living angel, to be alive and spirit. Her life was to serve others and deny, in essence kill, her physical wants and desires. For the men in her life, the woman's ultimate beauty laid in the fact that she was the passive object upon which he could write his ideal story. She did not act, but was acted upon. The fact that the women were no longer able to act made them less threatening. Envisioning women as passive beings kept the male fear of their own immortality, "that behind every so-called seductive temptress lies a grinning skull to haunt the onlooker" at bay (Bassein 35). In essence, wrapped up in the body and spirit of woman was both death and love for her lover.

In representing the dead woman, authors found a freedom in that by "being so excessively obvious…they escape observation in presenting a culturally familiar but deadly topic" (Bronfen, *Over* 3). These depictions give male viewers the ability to sustain a prolonged gaze at an object of desire in a respectable setting and, in turn, makes the dead the Other. The woman is on display in a place and setting that would have been socially unacceptable if she was not dead. Artistic representations of dead women remove the realities of death and replace them with the beauty of art. Yet, these images, along with the depictions of dead women in literature, lead to the marginalization of females (Bronfen, *Over* 59). The dead woman becomes the ultimate subject by becoming the site where "the unsettling exchange between figural and literal meanings…occur[s] when representations of 'femininity' and 'death' are at issue" (Bronfen, *Over* 59).

The images of the dead woman range from violent depictions to showing the beauty found in her dead body. In showing the dead woman as beauty, death becomes love. So many readings of the dead woman are available because "the dead body is...passive...while the survivor stands erect, imbued with a feeling of superiority" (Bronfen, *Over* 65). While in this position, the survivor is able to write his own story on the dead body, thus moving love and death into the realm of the ideal. Perhaps it is because the equation of women and death is so ingrained that it has kept scholars from investigating Wharton's depiction of the interaction of love and death.

Wharton's works negotiate between the philosophical and scientific views that were prevalent during her life and found in her reading. Scholars have shown how she experimented with many forms of the novel ranging from bildungsroman to sentimental to realism (Hoeller x, Miller Hadley 4). They have also found that passion is detrimental for women, resulting either in form death or utter disillusionment (Hadley 138, Dyman 47). Marriage does not fare much better than passion in Wharton's fictional world (Dimock; Lewis; White; Wolff, *Feast*). Because of this negative view on marriage, many find Wharton's works dark (Allen 34). Although this darkness may be true of her early works, in her later works characters often find one person with whom they are able to find a balanced love. This person, as it turns out, is their ideal soul mate; the one with whom they are to make their perfect union. In her final work, the happiest depiction of love is found with Nan being able to find a fulfilling union of physical and soul love. Yet, in all of their studies, no one has looked at Wharton's comprehensive philosophy about love across her works. That philosophy, I would argue, fluctuates between believing in her early works that spiritual love should prevail but that it could only be found in the realm beyond life, to the prevalence of physical love in the works from the middle of her career. It was only, in *The Buccaneers*, that Wharton truly came to terms with both spiritual love and physical love on earth. She eventually works out a solution between love and death through her theories of beyond and beyondness. Yet, because her last work was left unfinished, we do not know exactly how she would have worked out her final word on this theory. From the part of the novel that we do have, we can see that there is a happy tone to her final work that does not appear in any of her early works.

In discussing the types of love Wharton presents in her works, I have stayed away from using the term *Platonic love* because today the term has taken on a meaning unintended by Plato (Waterfield). Although Platonic love is still a spiritual love, the term has become more closely related to love between friends, than a love between soul mates. Often, I use the terms *soul love* and *spiritual love* interchangeably. This is not to imply that the love of the souls is only a religious or spiritual element, as in *agape* and *caritas*. However, by using the term *spiritual love*, I mean the love of one spirit or soul for another's spirit or soul.

The books I have selected for this study range across Wharton's career from one of her earliest works, "The Fullness of Life" to her final work *The Buccaneers*. They were selected because they were representative works and views from different periods of her career. Scholars have treated some of the novels selected as inferior works. I hope to show that these books, when analyzed in light of the conflict between love and death are not inferior. In the chapters that follow, I will trace the conflict between Eros and Thanatos throughout Wharton's career. Much like in life, the struggle is ever present in her depiction of romantic relationships with Thanatos being more dominant at times and with Eros being dominant at other times. After reading "The Fullness of Life" as the key to Wharton's depiction of the struggle, we move into the depiction of the battle in two of her early novels, *The House of Mirth* (1905) and *The Fruit of the Tree* (1907), where she holds the spiritual love found in death to be the ideal. I elected to begin with *The House of Mirth* instead of *The Valley of Decision* (1902), because *The Valley of Decision* is the only historical novel Wharton wrote. As such, it is a departure from her core works and a vehicle allowing her to focus on political issues, instead of romance. Although there are elements of the struggle found in her historical novel, it is such an aberration from her opus that it is obvious she was working with a different intention in writing the historical novel. *The House of Mirth* is essential because it establishes the Republic of the Spirit, a place beyond, where knowing souls can find an ideal spiritual union without the bonds of the physical. This Republic, along with its counterpart the faux Republic, becomes a core embodiment of her views of love.

In selecting *The Fruit of the Tree*, I hope to show how some of the negative views on the novel are resolved once we turn our focus of analysis to the conflict between love and death. This early period culminates with perhaps one of Wharton's most death-filled works, *Ethan Frome* (1911). After this dark point, Wharton's middle works show that she found her solution of spiritual love in death to be suspect. The conflict is perhaps the strongest in *The Reef* (1912), where death is in the background and the two women with whom George Darrow has relationships are in conflict in their conception of love. For Sophy the physical love is the entrance to a deeper union, but for Anna the physical love Darrow felt for another corrupts her version of an ideal spiritual love, leaving her to either give him up or revise her notion of love.

With *Summer* (1917), the companion piece to *Ethan Frome*, we see a dramatic change in Wharton's ideas about honoring the physical. This work is the first where Wharton considers physical love as the ideal love and the way to enter into a love of souls. With this novel and her later works, there is a turn towards a lightness not found in her earlier works. *The Glimpses of the Moon* (1922) shows steps, albeit tentative steps, towards Wharton being able to envision a complete union for her characters in life. Yet, Wharton follows this work with her most cynical depiction of love in *Twilight Sleep* (1927). It is in this work that no form of love is seen as beneficial and the lead character is left with no love to believe in. Finally, Wharton's last work, *The Buccaneers* (1938), was chosen for this study because it was her final word on the conflict she saw as dominating love and death. Not only is it her final word on the topic, but it is also her happiest novel in that the characters appear to be able to find spiritual love not beyond, but in life through an acknowledgement of the ability to see beyond life, the ability to recognize Platonic ideals in life.

CHAPTER TWO

"The Fullness of Life"

The key to Wharton's philosophy on love and death can be found in her early work, "The Fullness of Life." This short story, first published in *Scribner's Magazine* in December, 1893, provides the key to her contradictory views regarding love. Burlingame, her publisher, thought the "dialogue too 'soulful'" and requested a rewrite, but Wharton refused, returning the work with only one sentence changed (Benstock 72). Wharton herself considered the story to be among the group of stories that "were all written 'at the top of my voice'" (Lewis, *Letters* 36). She continues to describe it as "one long shriek. —I may not write any better, but at least I hope to write in a lower key, & I fear that the voice of those early tales will drown all the others" (Lewis, *Letters* 36). Many scholars have interpreted Wharton's reference to this "shriek" as an indication that she had revealed too much of her personal life in the story (Lewis; Benstock; Wolff, *Feast*). While the story may have some parallels to her life, Wharton's concern regarding it could also reveal her thinking that the depiction of her views on love was too obvious. In any case, Wharton refused to have the stories republished in her 1899 collection, *The Greater Inclination* (Lewis, *Letters* 36).

Wharton's concern about these stories is quite interesting, considering that scholars have tended to dismiss them. It seems that scholars linking this story to her life have only responded to parts of "The Fullness of Life," not the entire work. By focusing on the interaction of love and death in the story, Wharton struggles with diverging notions of love, physical and spiritual, trying to discover which is most desirable. This short story is the most explicit and overt representation of the questions regarding love that are Wharton's focus throughout her career.

For our purposes, physical love is one that abides by Darwinian sexual selection and desire. In other words, this love focuses upon the physical attributes that attract mates to each other. In *Descent of Man*, Darwin points out that the selection of certain physical/material aspects creates an ideal standard of beauty that is passed down from generation to generation for each culture. Spiritual love is Plato's idealized love. In the *Symposium*, Socrates' speech defines love as the halfway point between "mortality and immortality" (43). Love becomes the love of one soul for another in seeking goodness and beauty. Because of this view of love, platonic love becomes the ideal, while Eros becomes passionate desire that can have negative effects on a person (xxxii). It is a union of like minds that focus on beauty and other aesthetic matters. In Wharton's early works this is the type of love that the characters seek as the ideal at the expense of physical love.

The most common scholarly treatment of "The Fullness of Life" claims that the story is an illumination of Edith's unhappy marriage to Edward "Teddy" Wharton. Because Teddy was not her first choice in a mate, and because of her affair with Morton Fullerton and subsequent divorce from Teddy, scholars have focused on the notion that the story was an expression of Wharton's frustrations with him. The parallels between the story and Wharton's life caused her, according to this reading, to refuse to revise it for Scribner's and are the reason she refused to include it in her first collection of stories (Lewis, Wolff). Auchincloss (65–66), Benstock (71) and Craig (81), among others, have made similar comments. Yet, this work, which scholars often dismiss as an example of Wharton's inferior writing, has one of the most often quoted passages in Wharton scholarship that equates a woman's character to the rooms of a house (14). Although there are some rooms that receive visitors, there are many rooms that do not. In fact, there is one room, where the soul waits, alert for the sound of the one person who can reach it. However, those footsteps are never heard. For many scholars, this selection is the most eloquent expression of Wharton's views of a woman's nature. It seems strange to find such a penetrating passage for Wharton's view on women, which scholars consider to be so insightful, from a work deemed inferior by those same critics. In fact, this passage is the most overt description of the female psyche that we find in Wharton's works.

It is not my intention here to discount the potential links between this story and Wharton's life or the traditional explanation of the story as the conflict between self and society. I do believe, however, that if one reads the story in terms of a woman learning about life, love, and herself through death, the story becomes a richer and a less inferior work. Ironically, the story is about a woman who can truly learn about how full her life was only when she is dead. In death, she can discover her voice to express her unhappiness in life, to discover her love and desires. She has to be dead to find love, albeit an imperfect love, yet a love that had been available to her all along. In addition, it is while she is dead that she can experience an alternate love to the physical love that her husband provided. Whether as a result from her own unhappy and unfulfilled marriage or the author's creative vision, Wharton uses the characters in "The Fullness of Life" to depict a world where women can only find love in the afterlife. In other words, there is no place for love in life for a woman. She can only find love in the world beyond: in death.

"The Fullness of Life" depicts a woman who, in her afterlife, tells the Spirit of Life that she never had the full life for which she had hoped. After hearing her case, the Spirit tells her that because she had not found her soul mate in life, she will meet him in death. Also, since they were not united in life, they would be together for eternity in death. After a few moments with her soul mate, the man asks her if she would like to depart from the threshold and begin their (after)life together. She is immediately reminded of her living husband. Upon learning from the Spirit that her earthly husband thought she was his soul mate, she decides to sit at the threshold to wait for him.

Wharton presents the woman's life before her death in brief flashes parallel to the brief moments of fullness the woman believed she experienced while alive. However, these scattered hints reveal how unequal she felt her desires were from those of her husband. Moreover, for the majority of the story her marriage appears to be as unfulfilled as she imagines. In the opening deathbed scene the incompleteness of her life reveals itself through her feelings for her husband. Her death is "a seductive and sensually beckoning portrait of death—of letting go, ceasing to struggle, allowing oneself to be swallowed up by…total passivity" (Wolff, *Feast* 70). In a way, it is the woman's goodbye to the physical, erotic love and her introduction into the spiritual union that could await her beyond. Instead of worrying about missing her husband, remembering the good times they had together or her husband surviving without her, she feels relieved that she will no longer have to contend with physical irritants such as taking medicine and hearing her husband's noisy boots. In these final moments of life she focuses on the negative, instead of any positive aspects of her life. The mundane physical elements of her life and her relationship with her husband annoy and occupy her last thoughts. More specifically, it is the relief from the extreme physicality that satisfies her.

Perhaps this focus on the physical is why the woman mentions Darwin, Wallace, and Mivart almost immediately upon entering the afterlife. In essence, in invoking these names she is contemplating the differences between a physical and spiritual life and love. She is happy when the afterlife proves not to be the end, as Darwin's theory of evolution would imply it to be. She does admit to believing in Darwin's scientific theories, "but then Darwin himself said that he wasn't sure about the soul…and Wallace was a spiritualist; and then there was St. George Mivart" (13). These three scientists present the three kinds of love that the woman will discover in her afterlife. Darwin, of course, with his predominantly physical view of the world, expresses the view of love that she thought she had while alive. It was a love based on selecting attractive traits to further the species. Evolution and sexual selection essentially remove all romantic notions of love from the relationship. There is no such consideration of a soul mate in these matches because evolution made God an artificial construct and based love on aesthetic selections. Mates did not care if they had a mental and spiritual union with each other, but were selected based on physical attributes.

Wallace represents the ideal love she hopes to find in the afterlife with her husband. He believed in the tenets of evolution. In fact, his work forced Darwin to publish his theories sooner than Darwin had planned on doing (Berry). Yet, in his later life, Wallace believed that natural selection could not account for all the changes that occurred to man. After attending his first séance in 1865, "it is likely that this new interest [in spiritualism] influenced his biology, and by 1869 he was willing to state publicly that he believed that more than natural selection was involved in the evolution of humans" (Berry 17). By the end of his life, natural selection became the "mechanism" of his "teleological" world-view (Berry 17). It is this view of life and love that the woman is waiting for at the end of her story. She is looking for a mingling of the spiritual and the physical that Wallace applied to his version of evolution. She is searching for a balanced love.

The reference to Mivart would be the extreme opposite of Darwin. In fact, Mivart was a critic of Darwin's theory in his claims that a process called individuation brought on by a divine power endowed man with intellect. He saw the difference between divine creation and natural selection to be important. Thus Darwin's failing, according to Mivart, was confusing natural selection with God's creation. In essence, Mivart placed the soul or the spiritual over the material creation. Wharton expresses this view in describing the love the woman experiences with her soul mate. He has no past because he is all soul. Any union with the soul mate would be a purely spiritual union. The body is not the primary concern in the afterlife, and, in fact, is of no concern at all.

Once the woman encounters the Spirit of Life, she explains that by society's standards, her life was not as unfulfilled as she thought it was. In fact, she acknowledges that other people thought them to be a completely happy and satisfied couple. Despite public opinion, however, she felt her husband did not understand her true nature. She blames this lack of understanding on her husband because he was incapable of admiring the same things she did; after all, he reads railway novels. In other words, they did not understand each other because she was concerned with the higher spiritual pursuits to which he was blind. Her interest in love in life, therefore, was not a physical connection, but a spiritual connection

Wharton refines this lack of understanding in later works into the lack of a shared language to convey feelings and emotions. Because of this lack of a shared language and shared interests, the woman believes she did not have a happy, complete life. Interestingly, when pushed to explain her concept of the full life she thought she was missing, she does not connect any one single person to the experience, but connects the fullness to aesthetic moments of bliss. To connect with a person would mean to connect with the material side of things, yet to connect with beauty or the past is to find the spiritual connection in all things. To connect with the aesthetic moment is, according to Plato, her soul's way of seeking the ideal love. By seeking the beauty in all things, her soul is rejecting Eros in favor of a platonic, spiritual communion.

Because she equates her husband with the physical earthly realm, as evidenced by the constant references to the sound of his boots, her complaints with him revolve around his deep connection to the physical realm and lack of interest in the spiritual realm. He becomes the epitome of the physical in that he slams doors, his boots make too much noise, and he reads mundane novels. Even when they are in the church together, she experiences a spiritual communion while he is worried about returning to the hotel in time to dine. The worldly concerns that seem to be the focus of the husband's life are in direct opposition to the woman's otherworldly concerns.

He is centered in the earthly realm, while she is attracted to the realm beyond. She is more interested in the philosophical matters regarding the soul's union with the past and aesthetics. In essence, while they were alive, she thought he was seeking only her physical side while she was seeking a greater communion with the ideal.

It is evident that the woman thought she desired a complete physical and spiritual union in her life from her example of the fullness of life that she shares with the Spirit. While in the church she connects with the past in a way she had never done before as she was carried away on a "current" which had its beginning in the "beginning of things, and whose tremendous waters gathered as they went all the mingled streams of human passion and endeavor" (15). This beginning of her trip to awakening combines the physical nature of things with the water analogy and the spiritual nature of things in the streams of "passion" and "endeavor." Her moment of fulfillment takes her back to ideals (16) and carries her forward through the Middle Ages, martyrs, and Dante. It is this deep connection with the past that allowed her to become part of a group that united her with spirit and passion. This uniting the past with the present, the physical toils with the spiritual sacrifices of martyrs, which the woman was seeking on earth.

However, just as she was experiencing this ideal moment in her life, her husband misses it. He is more concerned with the material needs of the moment and is not tied to the past that she feels. He does not experience the exalted connection with the universe that she does, yet she cannot explain what he is missing to him. It does appear that even her husband realizes he is missing something important to her as he sat next to her. His only way to try to reunite with her is to make her return to the physical realm. The return to the physical, however, is too jarring for her given the fact that she had reached such heights of communion with the universe. What the woman refuses to recognize is that her husband is beckoning her to his love. He is trying to reunite with her the only way he knows how, through the physical.

The husband's attempt to reunite with his wife does point towards the conclusion of the story. Her husband waited for her to return from the spiritual union in the church just as she waits for him to join her in the afterlife. Although he did not feel the same spiritual union she experienced, his physical presence when she returned is a demonstration of his devotion to her. It is a sign of their shared past and what she means to him. This view of the past is in direct opposition to her spiritual lover's connection, or lack thereof, with his past. Her lover has forgotten his past which she cannot bring back for him. In forgetting his past, her spiritual lover has declared his past dead and, in a sense, repressed it. The man has put a definitive end to his history by forgetting it, thus there is no future for him to write with the woman. Her husband, on the other hand, has the physical past and she believes that by waiting for him in the afterlife he will find her and her spiritual side. He may not truly understand her, or what she is trying to show him, but they will have a past upon which to build together. There is the hope that he will eventually understand her enough to reach her soul.

It is only in death that the woman is able to voice this desire for a union with the past. Perhaps this is why her death scene reads more like a rebirth or the birth of a child. She softly rests until contractions of pain pass through her. As she travels closer to her birth into death, she feels death holding her until her body is submerged to the point of her feeling a choking feeling and breathlessness. Instead of the doctor treating her like a newborn baby, the nurse closes her eyes and the reader is left to see her husband's grief and her first steps as a newborn into the afterlife. It is only because her death is truly a rebirth that the Spirit of Life greets her. In effect, the spirit gives her a second chance at life in death. Her end, it seems, is a form of resurrection into love and life through death.

In the realm beyond the physical, the Spirit of Life grants her reparation in the form of finally meeting her soul mate because that is the repayment for those who live what they perceive to be an unhappy life. It is at this point that she finally meets her kindred soul. She cannot see his face so their meeting and conversation is on a purely spiritual level. In fact, his material appearance does not matter at all because his soul takes precedence over his physical appearance. The fact that she focuses on his soul serves to further differentiate him from her husband, trapped in the material. The woman and her soul mate's initial conversations, which center on great art and literature, fulfill her fantasy of a great intellectual union with another. Not only do they finish each other's sentences, but they also have a complete union of thoughts and feelings on aesthetic topics. This kind of relationship is often described as the ideal love relationship. She finally has a man whom she understands and who understands her. Scholars who do acknowledge the spiritual union concept in this story deem it a "questionable ideal" (Fedorko 17) or a sign of Wharton's "complete inability to represent a convincingly adult relationship between the sexes" (Wolff, *Feast* 70). Wolff finds that "this is not a relationship, it is an image of total oneness, fusion, a complete (and infantile) identification. It conjures no image of passion" (*Feast*, 70). That lack of physical passion, however, is precisely what Plato upheld as the ideal. He replaced the lack of physical passion, Eros, with the completeness of a matching beautiful soul.

However, once the lover tries to bring their relationship away from the spiritual realm into the physical realm of the home, she begins to have second thoughts. It is only then that the woman realizes that home is with her husband in the physical realm. In fact, she even admits that home would not be home without all the physical trappings and noises of her husband. In other words, unless her soul mate became the man her husband was it would not feel like home. It is not just the material ties that keep her with her husband; it is also the shared past that they have. This should not be surprising considering that even when she was alive, her fondest moment of the fullness of life connected her with the past, the present and the future in the church. Her soul mate, however, has forgotten all the other loves he had on earth. In essence, he has no past and no physical connection to Eros. Once she learns of his severed link to the past, she is freed from the romantic spell of their union to question the Spirit regarding her husband.

Hearing that her husband thought she was his soul mate forces her to seriously reconsider her life. Interestingly, this revelation causes the woman to cry out, a cry that she is unable to classify immediately. Was it a cry of unhappiness because he loved her so deeply, because she did not realize how much he loved her or because she did not love him as much as he loved her? Or did she feel happiness for so deeply touching his soul, even if he did not touch hers to the same depth? Alternatively, at this point, does she begin to realize that he may have touched her soul deeper than she thought? One must determine that for oneself. For the reader, this mention of the woman being her husband's soul mate gives his actions at her deathbed a new meaning. We must reconsider what the woman revealed throughout the story. His blindness at her death, which had taken on the meaning of his blindness to her needs in life, now is not just his misunderstanding her, but reflects his grief at losing her. He is lost and unable to see the world without his soul mate. Moreover, Wharton forces the reader to wonder about the extent to which the woman was blind to his needs and desires.

It is only after learning that she was her husband's soul mate that she decides to wait for her husband. Several scholars have interpreted this to show that she has chosen to relinquish her socially unsanctioned desires for the socially sanctioned marriage and draw the obvious parallels to the Wharton's marriage. Interestingly, the woman's reasons for the sacrifice are the physical claims that annoyed her about her husband earlier. She asserts that she is the only one who can take care of his mundane physical needs such as selecting his novels. In other words, she elects to wait for him in the realm beyond because he could not take care of his physical life without her. She realizes how connected to his physical life she was, but she can only see this connection in death. Once she has this realization she finally believes he would be completely lost without her in the afterlife. Although the Spirit tells her not to assume that her husband would not be happy without her, she refuses to believe the Spirit. She elects to make her husband happy and sacrifice her spiritual ideal for him. It appears that she is finally beginning to open her eyes regarding her husband and his love.

Having made her decision to stay, she says goodbye to her soul mate in the language of parting lovers. She tells him that another soul will come along to make him happy, yet that seems to be a strange sentiment to convey to one's soul mate. If they were truly soul mates, there could not be another soul mate for either person. This leaves the reader to wonder who the woman's true soul mate is: her husband or her lover. The woman, however, is not concerned about the man she meets in the afterlife because he has already proven he can forget the past, especially past lovers. The woman, however, is forever tied to her past. She will not forget. In fact, she does not want to forget her past.

The story's conclusion ties into Wharton's description of a woman's character mentioned earlier. She is in the afterlife, sitting alone, waiting for the sound of her husband's boots. This ending emphasizes the cyclical nature of the story and the cyclical nature of life and love. Essentially, one can read the story as the story of a woman going through the rooms of her own nature/house to end up as her own soul waiting. She needs to step through the rooms in order to learn about herself, her life, and her loves. Unfortunately, this is a trip she can only make in death, not life. Although the woman does chose the physical relationship she experienced with her husband, the ending of the story is not a truly happy conclusion. Wharton leaves the reader wondering what, if anything, has changed. The Spirit has warned her that her husband will not change, so the question is whether the woman has changed. Most likely, she does see things a little differently upon learning that she was her husband's soul mate. This is a lesson she can only learn in death. Ironically, the woman needs to be dead to appreciate and understand the fullness of her lived life. The ending, however, shows that she has a different appreciation for her life and has faith that her husband will find her innermost room. Her living hope to find her soul mate is overridden by other elements, such as the desire to be connected with the past and caring for her husband, which enable her to chose her husband over the mate offered by the Spirit of Life. There is also the hope that her husband will find her in the afterlife. In coming to terms, albeit only in death, with the physical love her husband offered her in life, the woman can make a parallel connection that her husband's death will allow him to come to terms with the spiritual love she desires. However, at the close of the story, her husband has neither returned nor acknowledged her new love. Instead she is left alone, waiting in eternity for her mate in the Republic of the Spirit. Yet, her belief in his ability to find her because of their shared experience is strong enough to make her happy in her wait.

Thus the story becomes a picture of the woman who could not find love in life but who found the prospect of love in death. The world of love that Wharton depicts here is bleak. At this point in her life Wharton sees Plato's version of spiritual love as the ideal, yet the woman cannot find that love in life. The only love available to the woman in life is a physical Eros based love. She cannot find fulfillment in life with Eros and, although she can find the fulfillment of spiritual love in death, she gives it up for the shared past of the physical. Without the shared physical past, the union with her soul mate is as unfulfilling as a purely physical love. Yet, this is only an understanding that the woman can find in death because her husband was unable to see beyond the physical in life, just as she was unable to see beyond the spiritual in life. However, her faith that her husband will have a similar understanding in death makes waiting for him a pleasant experience. There is hope for a future, greater love with her husband in death.

CHAPTER THREE

The House of Mirth

The theme of finding true love only through the death of one mate carries throughout Wharton's early work. *The House of Mirth*, much as "The Fullness of Life," is a novel where one mate must die before there is a true understanding of the love they shared in life. From Lily Bart's entrance in Grand Central Station to her exit in a rundown boarding house, Wharton reveals her to be a beautiful, romantic ideal. Her life is a series of material mistakes and offenses, but her death is a masterpiece.

For many scholars, this novel documents the rise and fall of one of Wharton's most popular characters, Lily Bart, whom society ruins. In support of this argument, they invoke Wharton's comment that the human element of her story comes from placing her heroine in a world where emotional attachments and romantic ideals are inferior to wealth. This world places more importance on money than on the value of love. Wharton sought to show how a woman who wanted to live by her high romantic ideals was discredited by those who could not live up to her standards. They believe that their relationships with others are just another trivial part of their lives, equal to living beyond their means, playing cards, and gossiping. In essence, these people who believe that life and relationships are just games to be played not only debase Lily's ideals, but ultimately lead to her death.

By focusing on the interaction of Eros and Thanatos throughout the novel, we see that Selden also has the tendency to believe that relationships are trivial as he attempts to play a game of love with Lily so that he can avoid, and perhaps even escape, a spiritual union with her. Instead of forming a more permanent bond with her, he indulges in the fantasy that he will be her rescuer, the one man who can make right all that is wrong in her life. In discussing *The House of Mirth*, some scholars have found love depicted as a single unified concept that wealth corrupts, yet that is not the case. Instead, Wharton presents three types of love relationships: sentimental experiments, monetary unions, and the ultimate union of like souls which one can find only in death. The sentimental experiment is the type of relationship that dominates Selden's life until he begins to play at the game of love with Lily. For Selden, the sentimental experiment is an inconsequential version of love. It allows for the people involved, Bertha and Selden, to play at the game of love while maintaining an emotional distance. They truly do not have any fondness for each other beyond the physical and have no intention of forming a more permanent union. Selden can be so careless with the letters from the women in these relationships because he feels no moral or emotional attachment to them. Instead, much as in the game of courtly love, these loves are meaningless physical adventures or games of love with women. They are not the stuff of which soul mates are made or revealed because it is a relationship that allows for the participants to toy with love without any investment of their true essence, their soul. These relationships are passing moments in the lives of those involved without long-term plans or complications.

The next step up from the sentimental experiment is the monetary union. This is the type of union that most scholars focus upon when describing how Wharton depicts society's destruction of Lily. By basing the monetary union upon the wealth of the participants, the "lovers" corrupt the notion of love for another soul. In the mind of the observers, and in most cases the participants, the matches are closer to business deals than love matches. Examples of this type of union abound throughout Wharton's novels. Lily's pursuit of Percy Gryce is a prime example. He is wealthy, but lacking the elements that Lily desires (19). Without wealth he would be unattractive. Yet, she spends the early part of the novel trying to entice him to marry her. In becoming his wife, she would have gained a bore of a husband who she does not love and who cannot provide for the needs of her soul, but who can provide her with monetary sustenance. It is because of this void that people in monetary relationships often partake in sentimental experiments in the hopes of finding what is missing in their current relationship, as in the case of Bertha Dorset.

The final relationship sought by the characters in *The House of Mirth* is the ideal spiritual union. This ideal union draws upon Plato's notion of love as a spiritual union of souls trying to unite with the ultimate good beauty. At this stage in her life and career, however, Wharton cannot conceive of this type of relationship being achieved in life. The other two types of love interfere with one soul meeting another in a loving union. Instead, spiritual love can only exist in the realm beyond the living, in what Selden calls the Republic of the Spirit. It is here that the participants are free from the corrupting influences of the world, of sentimental experiments and of monetary unions, to find a romantic, ideal form of love. Most often, the souls build this type of union on a like mind and a friendship that goes beyond the physical union and allows the participants a deeper love beyond. It is not necessarily a religious love, but a love that is not corrupted by physical, earthly love; it is a love found in the imagination. It is, as Selden eventually discovers, a type of love which becomes the center of the participants' world (121). This love is greater than just the two souls involved. Through their love for each other's soul, they are not only connected to each other's soul, but also to things beyond them and the world.

The Republic is a recurring theme throughout Wharton's works, but she does not necessarily refer to it by the same name. Instead, if one looks closely, one finds elements of it in various descriptions where there is a chance for lovers to meet in an ideal union, such as the feeling of flying high, or being above the rest of the world looking down upon them. It is a place where two souls with equal imagination can meet and share an ultimate spiritual connection. For Lily and Selden the entrance to the Republic is on the hilltop at Bellomont. Yet, as we shall see, they are unable to enter this realm while both are alive because Selden's pursuit of Lily fluctuates between the desire to make her into another sentimental experiment, as his relationships with Bertha and other women have been, and the desire to rescue her, which turns her into a burden instead of a soul mate. He does not have the faith and devotion of a true lover of her soul until her death; only then can he finally love her soul because she has gone beyond the earthly corruption. In fact, he is constantly torn between seeing her as an ideal woman and one of the more physical beings. Her pursuit of him, however, has the consistency of belief in seeking spiritual communion. It is because of her desire for this ultimate spiritual communion that she constantly rejects material unions with wealthy men such as Percy Gryce, or sentimental experiments with men like Gus Trenor.

It is not only New York Society that acts to destroy Lily's idealized notion of love, but also Selden's thinking of her as a sentimental experiment until she either appears dead or is actually dead, rather than as his soul mate that destroys her. However, her death finally enables him to envision a love for her beyond that of a sentimental experiment to a union of souls beyond earthly love. As Wershoven states, "Lily's death awakens Selden to his character and, at least in part, redeems him" (45). She is able to save him because her death forces him to see her as more than a passing fancy, more than a Darwinian physical mate, but as a soul mate in the realm beyond life. Thus, at this point in her writing, Wharton appears to believe that only death has the power to transform love from a sentimental experiment to a communion of like spirits.

Unfortunately, the people surrounding her cannot comprehend Lily's inability to form a monetary match which would enable her to pursue sentimental experiments of her own. They see her as still eligible to land a wealthy match, which would free her up to pursue trivial matches. They cannot recognize that she is unwilling to relinquish her desire for an ideal union based on a spiritual communion with one other soul. Yet, many scholars see Lily's concept of an ideal spiritual union as an attempt to avoid reality (Miller Budick; Schriber). At the foundation of this desire to avoid reality is a society that encourages its members to see women as commodities and beautiful objects. The society in which Lily and Selden find themselves rejects Plato's notion of a soul seeking love in a spiritual union with the good and beautiful in favor of physical and monetary matches. Instead of the soul seeking the good and beautiful, the good and beautiful must seek out the soul to love it.

Throughout the novel Lily has the option to participate in the socially approved material union, the sentimental experiment, and, eventually, an ideal spiritual union. Her inability to accept something less than her heart's desire, to repress her desire for a complete soul union, results from her being different from the rest of her social set. Her traits and desires have evolved beyond theirs which makes Selden realize that she is different from the others he has met. He imagines she is an idealized version of womanhood. She is more beautiful, more brilliant and more moral than the people in the environment in which Selden is accustomed to living as demonstrated in her actions regarding Bertha's letters. Lily is not only set apart by what she is as part of this society, but also by what she desires. She has the imagination to see something beyond the physical realm, to desire a spiritual union for herself and her mate. Those who are not members of Lily's race are willing to settle for the material, physical union and sentimental experiments instead of a union of souls. Lily becomes, in essence a philosopher-poet from Plato's Republic; she becomes an ideal.

As if to emphasize the conflict between Darwin's theory and Plato's ideals confronting Wharton and her characters, Selden accounts for Lily's beauty through a mysterious form of sexual selection. For Selden, at this point, it is predominantly her external features which make her different from the other women in his world. Despite the fact that she has the heredity, beauty and training to succeed in achieving a physical, monetary union, she consistently sabotages her achievements toward this socially sanctioned goal. Selden is aware that the analogy he creates to explain her differences is inadequate, but he is not ready or able to consider Lily's life and usefulness beyond the monetary union or experiment (7). In fact, his contemplation of her ceases the moment she leaves his line of sight. However, he does show promise at discovering that Lily can be, and is, something more than physical. He does understand that his attempt to classify her uniqueness is slightly off (7).

The Lily whom Selden describes is a prime specimen of and for Darwinian sexual selection. Her exterior encourages success in a society which honors physical, monetary unions. However, the material which created her was better and, therefore, her desires evolved in conjunction with her material evolution. This evolution of her desires is the driving force which enables her to seek a more fulfilling union. Lily recognizes that there is more to life and love than Eros and money, and she will not become a slave to Eros. Unfortunately, this desire for a more fulfilling, complete union has not developed in Lily's cohorts. To them, the sentimental experiment exists to fulfill the voids in monetary relationships. What the others lack, and Lily possesses, serves to isolate her from their tribe. Given that Lily possesses this specialized beauty and desires a complete spiritual union with another, she spends her life seeking a union based on Plato's ideals. Of all the available mates, she only considers one, Selden, to be specialized like her. Lily is quick to notice and identify Selden's specialization, just as he noticed hers. He has the physical beauty to be a perfect Darwinian match; he also has the ability to rise above the members of society (53). He is, in fact, capable of imaging and achieving the ideal soul-love that Lily seeks in life.

She realizes that not only does he have the specialized physical attributes equivalent to those he admires in her, but he also is superior to the rest of the people around him. He is above the richest man because of a past which enabled him to remain aloof. In order to raise him above the rest, she connects Selden to the past, just as the wife connected the husband to the past in "The Fullness of Life" and as will happen repeatedly throughout Wharton's works. Selden's past, however, may be very different from Lily's. Lily's is built up on a series of inferior people, but Selden receives the gifts of his past from unknown sources (53). These sources can be people, culture, and society, but Lily does not speculate on that. For Lily it is not what went into making the man that is important, but that he is better than the rest and, potentially capable of conceptualizing a spiritually ideal soul union.

Perhaps to foreshadow the direction their relationship will take the contrast between Eros and Thanatos is present in the descriptions of their specialized natures. As he contemplates her specialized nature, Selden posits that people have been sacrificed to create her. For Lily to exist, according to Selden, she must live off of the people in a potentially vampiric or parasitic sort of relationship. She shines as they fade into the background. The specialization he creates for her is a negation of life, built upon sacrifices. Lily, however, envisions Selden's specialized nature as gifts bestowed upon him so that he carries the marks of those who went before him. No one was sacrificed in Selden's creation. Instead, Selden receives his gifts in a positive manner, much as a higher being receives spiritual offerings. The link to the past is a key element in the depiction of Wharton's female characters' selection of an ideal mate. To have a beneficial connection with past generations is a form of an enduring relationship beyond a physical union. As we saw in "The Fullness of Life," this connection to the past is essential in recognizing a soul mate.

Wharton enhances the connection between life, death, and love throughout her description of their relationship. The moments when Lily is most alive and beautiful, however, are the moments when Selden likes her least. As Louis Auchincloss argues, "It is possible to read Lily's whole story in the changes of her appearance" (72). This not only applies to her life in society, but it can also assist in reading her love relationship with Selden. When she looks young and alive, in essence full of life, he equates her with an enslaving Eros. When "life" intrudes into their relationship, Selden experiences a strong disgust for her which is evident when he sees her leaving Trenor's house at night. In Selden's view of Lily, when she is most alive, she is most real, and, therefore, most sexual.

When Lily looks young and alive, Selden believes Eros dominates her and, therefore, sees her as one of those women interested in, and capable of, a sentimental experiment. Since he does not hold these relationships in high esteem, as evidenced by his carelessness with the ladies' letters, he does not hold Lily in high esteem when he believes she is capable of this sort of love. The essential element of these sentimental experiments is the lack of a deep soul communion with another. In a way, being involved in these relationships is like playing at love. Flirtation and devotion without emotional connection characterize these relationships. They are, as Richard Kaye points out, "a means by which Wharton's characters negotiate the distance between illegitimate desire and an acceptable social identity" (156). Interestingly enough, these sentimental experiments are only available for married people (124). For a single woman to participate in one of these relationships would not only be scandalous, but also ruinous of any future chances for her at a monetary union.

The dilemma for Lily begins at Grand Central Station when Selden characterizes her as a player in the game reserved for the wealthy married females. Yet, Lily is neither a married woman like Bertha, nor a divorced woman like Carry, and therefore is ineligible to play in the game without serious detriment to her soul and her reputation. In other words, if she were to partake of the privilege of these two classes of women to form sentimental experiments, she would be violating conventions. Selden, however, refuses to acknowledge this. When she appears young and alive, she is the same as all the other society women to him. When she is most alive, he believes she is a vehicle of Eros, instead of a potential soul mate. Thus, the central problem of their relationship becomes Selden thinking of her as part of the game while Lily is seeking a spiritual communion. He will never love her the way she wishes as long as he continues to think of her as this type of woman. Keeping her in mind as a sentimental experiment enables him to avoid seeing her as a "real" woman capable of being his soul mate. As long as she is alive, he refuses to see her in any other light.

Although Selden sees Lily as a sentimental experiment, Percy Gryce, on the other hand, sees her in terms of a monetary union. Despite her lack of money, Lily will make Gryce more valuable by being a beautiful addition to the things he owns. Lily's conquest of Gryce nears success until Selden's arrival, which forces her to compare Gryce to Selden, and, ultimately, to reject the material well-being which he offers. Unfortunately, Gryce's inferiority is brought to the forefront during this comparison (44). Even with all his money and Gryce Americana, he cannot provide Lily with the spiritual communion she seeks because he is intellectually incapable of envisioning a soul union. She realizes that his lack of higher thoughts would forever hinder him from reaching Selden's heights (18). He is incapable of imagining the higher things in life, things found beyond the physical realm which Lily and Selden both understand to exist.

Lily refuses to settle for a man with dull tastes who would forever remain oblivious to his banishment from the ultimate spiritual union. To settle, thus making a sacrifice of Gryce to create Lily's splendor, is beneath her. Although he can offer her material comforts, the riches which bought those comforts only serve to illuminate how lacking he is in other areas she desires such as imagination (45). In a society that honors material well-being, the only poverty that Gryce has is spiritual. His achievement is purely monetary. The closest he can come to any sort of soul is buying his way to the front of the church and donating to charities (47). He can imagine no better and believes these material trappings are the best life has to offer. Although in aligning herself with Gryce she would be beautiful, dressed in the finest clothes, and eligible for sentimental experiments, she would be sacrificing her ideal. This is why, when Selden arrives, Lily destroys all the progress she made toward a material union with Gryce. Selden's presence reminds her not to settle for the physical.

Once Selden arrives, Lily catches a glimpse into the realm she wishes to inhabit. As she becomes increasingly convinced that the ideal spiritual union is what she desires, Selden becomes increasingly confused. He insists in keeping one foot in the material realm and the other in the spiritual realm. They both recognize this split. In essence, he is, at this point, unable to commit fully to a singular world view or to a singular view of Lily. He is torn between the view of her as a sentimental experiment and a romantic idealized love in need of rescuing. When she is most life-like, most associated with Eros, she becomes part of a game-playing society. When she becomes closer to death, he is more willing to see her as a romantic ideal. As Lily comes closer to death, she becomes closer to his ideal soul mate. For Selden to love Lily, "she must be beautiful, all the while appearing to be above material concerns" (Wolff, "Lily" 27). The only way for Lily to fulfill these requirements is in death.

Yet, before her death, it is obvious that she does wish to create a deeper union with him while on the ledge at Bellomont. It is while they are in this "zone of lingering summer" that Lily and Selden try to come to a deeper understanding of each other through approaching the threshold of the Republic, both verbally and spiritually (51). Lily's ideal realm has no name until Selden utters it. However, once he speaks, she feels that he has read her thoughts and this allows her to hope for a deeper connection with him. His ability to name her idealized realm encourages Lily to believe that she has found a like mind. After all, if he can speak of their Republic, he must know how to get there and understand it. Selden, on the other hand, only has a shaky grasp of the topic himself. He knows that to be there is a sign of "success" and "personal freedom," but he believes it is a place to discover alone (55). His choice of the word "success" is quite interesting considering that earlier he told Lily that true success was a finding her (50). Perhaps their being so near and yet so far away in their conceptualization of their realm stems from their different mindsets approaching the discussion. Leading up to the discussion, Selden is so preoccupied with the material and physical side of life that once on the ledge, he is happy to relax in the physical beauty and warmth of the lingering summer without conversation. His preference is for the physical over the mental and spiritual at this time. His mind is on earthly pleasures at the expense of a more complete spiritual union.

Lily, however, is focused on the mental and spiritual, the inward feelings and emotions. She "was throbbing inwardly with a rush of thoughts. There was in her at the moment two beings, one drawing deep breaths of freedom and exhilaration, the other gasping for air in a little black prison-house of fears. But gradually the captive's gasps grew fainter, or the other paid less heed to them: the horizon expanded, the air grew stronger, and the free spirit quivered for flight" (52). Lily's split selves divide into the spiritual being drawing breaths of freedom and the material being trapped in its prison house. As she moves from the material into the society of Selden's newly named world, she relinquishes the material for her desired soul-communion.

It is only in Selden's presence that her soul can grasp the freedom it needs to survive and grow. That Lily's thoughts of love only occur when this self has been unleashed this emphasizes that love, for Lily, is not simply a material union, but a spiritual communion of like minds. In previous meetings, she had found him physically attractive, but never really considered loving him until they are on the hill together. During their time on the hill, Lily examines her feelings for Selden, especially since she had never felt this way with anyone else before. She admits to herself that she understands and knows why she feels so connected to him at this moment (52). Lily decides that what she feels with Selden is not just primitive sexuality. Instead, it is a feeling which gives her the freedom of being with someone with whom she has a deeper bond. In other words, the feeling is beyond the physical union that most people experience. It is something greater, something that flows back to the past and, potentially, into their future together, if both are willing and able to recognize it. It is important to note, as in "The Fullness of Life," that this bond with the past is included in her concept of love. Yet, at this point, only Lily is able to understand it in terms of the deep connection she feels for him and the knowledge that it is different with Selden than with any other man. She is able to realize that this difference emphasizes a deep link to each other and a freedom from material concerns.

Selden, oblivious to her thoughts, persists in seeing her as superficially as possible (53). Unfortunately, this is in direct opposition to Lily's feelings. She has moved beyond being a specimen of physical beauty in his presence and is truly seeking a communion of souls. Her lack of scheming should make her successful in appealing to his spirit. She knows she is a failure in what should be her ultimate goal: marrying money. It is only when discussing the Republic of the Spirit that they come to an agreement as to what success means to them both. Lily quickly gives up her initial definition of success as material pursuits, something she never really accepted in the first place, when she feels a moment of connection to him through his words. Selden's explanation of success recalls Lily's definition of love. For him, success is a kind of freedom, which includes independence "from everything—from money, from poverty, from ease and anxiety, from all the material accidents. To keep a kind of republic of the spirit" (55). The freedom from material pursuits is appealing to Lily, who has only a small sum of money. Despite his explanation of success and its vocabulary which is strikingly similar to her conception of love, Selden sees the Republic as a solitary place. To Selden, at this point, the Republic exists only as "a romantic escape from the society surrounding him" (Joslin, *Wharton* 68). His Republic is a way for him to escape reality. Since he elects not to see beyond the immediate social pressures inflicted on him, he sees the Republic as a place for individuals only. Lily, however, seeks companionship in the

Republic and, in fact, realizes that it takes more than one person on a solitary pursuit to enter. Selden's definition of success as love in the realm of spiritual communion is what encourages Lily to feel they have a union of agreement and understanding.

Selden's belief that the idealized realm must be discovered alone demonstrates he does not fully understand the concept of a soul mate at this point (55). He has had, in fact, a fear of becoming emotionally connected to Lily beginning with their time together in his apartment with her. To allow an emotional connection with her would mean to feel something for her beyond the physical, which is something he is unwilling to acknowledge while she is alive. Instead, he persists in the delusion that he must spend his life rescuing her (6). In persisting with this belief of being her champion, he does not see her as an equal partner capable of love, but indulges in a sentimental fantasy regarding her. Yet, he fails to rescue her from numerous social deaths and from the corrupted version of love that eventually leads to her death. If she can find the ideal world without his help, then maybe he will consider her, but that is the best he is willing to offer her at this point. By asking for his help, she begins to show him that they need each other to reach their ideal world and ideal love in the realm beyond the real. She tells him that he is incorrect in thinking that one must find the Republic oneself. She admits, "I should never have found my way there if you hadn't told me" and "Whenever I see you, I find myself spelling out a letter of the sign—and yesterday—last evening at dinner—I suddenly saw a little way into your republic" (55). This, in essence, is her way of telling him that he is the key to her happiness, that he is her soul mate. She is sending him a letter of the sign she wishes him to read. He is the only one, if willing, who has the imagination to join her in the rarer air of the Republic.

At this outburst from Lily, Selden realizes she has changed. She is no longer the premeditating, manipulative woman trying to break into the wealthy social set. She is no longer worthy of just being a sentimental experiment. Instead, she has a weakness which makes Selden desire her even more (55). Interestingly, while he thinks of her as weak, he imagines it is how she looked in the morning, when she is alone and her true self is able to show through (55). It is when he sees the weakened and pale Lily that he fears that they have reached the point of no return (55). This is troubling to him because he is seeing Lily's true feelings. He believes that she is acting against the plan she should be following in life by demonstrating her love for him. No matter what he tries to tell himself, he thought it gratifying to know she would modify her course for him (55). He has finally seen her without airs, seen her unguarded, and no longer understands how to relate to her other than to ask if she will be joining the people in the Republic (55). He sees that she truly does need his assistance and he is the only one who can rescue her. In saving her, as we shall soon see, he not only would gain a beautiful wife, as Perseus gained when he rescued Andromeda, but he also believes he would gain a deadly burden.

Only when she has turned from the lively beauty of the hike to the pale woman of the morning is he able to recognize that they both have feelings for each other (55). Selden cannot, or will not, ever love her while she is alive. To love her while she is alive is to admit to and love her erotic side. It is a chance for Eros to be an enslaving force. It is only when she is pale and death-like that he acknowledges his love for her. This is just the first instance of his love for her revealing itself as she turns from a living to a dead woman. Selden's feelings for her becoming something other than his normal amusement startle him (58). He never would have imagined spending time with her like this because their conversation became too intimate. He cannot accommodate the idea of Lily as his soul mate, instead of a calculating woman. Instead, he had expected to keep their afternoon on the level of the sentimental experiment with no emotional ties.

Before their afternoon is over, "they seemed lifted into a finer air. All the exquisite influences of the hour trembled in their veins, and drew them to each other" (59). They have finally found that rarer society that only the two of them can find. Despite all intervening factors, their finding the way together was inevitable. Both of their souls found each other and that drew them into the Republic. Although this is an idealized romantic notion of love and lovers, it is what the two of them need. For one brief moment, they are free from the social obligation and restrictions that press upon them, and they allow their real selves to emerge. Finding the higher air is just as inevitable as the effects of gravity on the leaves for the two of them. Only rare, specialized beings like Selden and Lily can find their way into the Republic, beyond the artifice of life. For Selden, however, this new world is too much for him to act upon, forcing him to deny their new world and return to reality (59). Accompanying his return is the desire to show her how unaffected by the whole event he was (59). He cannot let her see that the flight has touched him as much as it has touched her. To do that would be to admit that she is more to him than a sentimental experiment. To admit his feelings for her while she is alive would mean that he would have to become part of the world, instead of just a spectator in it. Selden holds his pride in being a spectator to life too dear to let it go.

Lily, however, does not recover as quickly and as solidly as Selden from their flight. Instead she was left faintly shaking (59). She has glimpsed the place of her ideal soul-love in the world beyond and the shock back to reality is too harsh for her. She truly is shaken more than either she or Selden is willing to admit. Yet her final words suggest the true meeting of their adventure on the hill. She questions if he was serious in his desire to marry her, her voice betraying her desire for the answer to be yes, but he is under the control of the real and wounds her with his response. In essence, this scene creates the beginning of a moment of understanding for them of the new world they could inhabit if they elected to do so. Despite lacking the prime elements honored in the material union, they could succeed if they chose to help each other find the Republic of the Spirit, which means so much to both of them. Unfortunately, Selden is too afraid to make the commitment to help Lily find her way there because he still believes she is not his equal. The notion of the spiritual union had, during their discussion, surprised him. However, he had the imagination and skill to see the delights that world offered.

It is more difficult for Lily to recover from this moment, because it was a moment nearing the spiritual love she desires. In fact, she never fully recovers from her flight into the rarer air of their new world and that knowledge of the realm colors all her future actions. When she meets up with him again, is saddened by his not acknowledging what happened between them on the hilltop (75). She tries to overcome his resistance by becoming the weak woman she was when they first took flight into the beyond at Bellomont. For a brief moment, it does work, until Gus Trenor and Simon Rosedale interrupt them and, by their presence, remind Selden of Lily's erotic side.

From this point until the Brys' party, Lily appears more alive in her beauty than ever. The physical description of her makes her sound like an ideal mate in a world of Darwinian sexual selection. She is described as looking fresher than ever before (89). Once again she is able to draw the eyes of all the men in the room to her and she seems to flourish in the attention. It would seem obvious to most that when she is most alive in her beauty, she would be most desirable to the males. She becomes the ideal mate based on physical traits. However, just as other men begin to find her most desirable, Selden finds her least desirable. He preferred Lily to be an idealized and romanticized love instead of the Darwinian physicality that the other men find desirable. It is not until the evening at the Brys' that she becomes something more to him. For her to complete the transition from sentimental experiment to soul mate, she needs to reach his imagination.

In order to accomplish this transition, Lily appropriates Reynolds's "dead beauty by the beams of her living grace" in the tableau vivante entertainment (106). Reynolds's painting commemorates the marriage of Joanna Leigh and Richard Bennett Lloyd (Penny 275). The picture shows a woman dressed in a gown cinched at the waist, clinging tightly to her legs, as she carves the name of her lover into a tree in the forest. Reynolds may have actually taken the pose of *Mrs. Lloyd* from "Raphael's famous drawing of *Adam Tempted*" (Penny 275). Nicolas Penny argues it was painted post engagement because she was carving Lloyd's name in the tree (275). Given that there are a significant number of copies, this painting was, most likely, very popular. Drawing upon the Italian Baroque "motif of a lady carving her true love's name on the bark of a tree," it plays into the romantic notion of true lovers throughout the ages (Penny 275). There is something essentially idealized and romantic in the depiction of the lover carving the beloved's name.

Lily, in her depiction of *Mrs. Lloyd*, causes a stir in the evening's entertainment. Judith Fryer argues that the scandal is not because of nudity or overt sexuality, since the previous depictions were based on paintings that revealed more. It is the fact that she uses her body as a point of convergence between the "classical goddess and the femme fatale" that is so scandalous to the men in the audience (Fryer 47). It is also, a frank and overt depiction of idealized and romanticized love for another. Elements of the tableau scene are reminiscent of the Republic of the Spirit scene, but instead of Lily feeling responsive toward a like mind, it is Selden who feels the bond with her. However, in the tableau Lily is not just Lily, she is impersonating someone else; she is impersonating a beautiful dead woman. Lily has created a physical approximation of the Republic without the emotional or imaginative connections. Lily, in the tableau, not only evokes a response from him, but she also is able to send him another signal as to how to reach the ideal realm (105).

The scene opens by emphasizing Selden's receptiveness to her creation (105). As a member of the specialized group, he believes he is receptive to the images the depictions are meant to convey. Selden still believing in her creation, finds it easier to let his guard down and to let the images seduce him. In these images the actors are living, yet passive. They are alive, yet not alive in their utter stillness. There is no change. The characters in these scenes are static, yet it is only the open mind that can receive their true meaning (105). The scenes are of women impersonating art to those who cannot truly see, but to a like mind, the living and the (dead) art become one. In fact, to Selden life, death and art merge in the tableaux. Although the participants are still alive in the living pictures, they relinquish the majority of the traits associated with the living. They are unable to move, to act, and to react. They are, in a sense, unchangeable, static, and death-like while in the tableau.

In Lily's tableau, the living Lily has performed the task of completely replacing Reynolds's Mrs. Lloyd with her form (106). In other words, the dead Mrs. Lloyd no longer exists; only Lily taking the place of the dead woman exists. In doing this, she takes her place in a long line of idealized, romantic lovers. She becomes the woman who "tempted Adam" along with the frivolous woman who is so consumed by love that she needs to carve her lover's name on every tree. Either of these should make her unappealing to Selden; however, that is not the case. Instead, she merges with the dead lovers to create a new fantasy for him. She is able to become his ideal. She is static, unchangeable, and finally worthy of his admiration because of it. It is while watching this pale version of her that he thinks he sees the real Lily, as he did when he saw her pale face earlier (106). Thus for Selden, the real Lily is a recipient of his idealized love, capable of great romantic feelings. Only when she is out of the actual, living world and part of the eternal world can he love her; only when Thanatos has overwhelmed Eros can he love her. It is then that she is idealized in his imagination and can no longer be a slave to Eros or threaten to make him a slave. She is the ideal soul-love because he can see her as a dead woman.

It takes this spectacle of idealized love and temptation for Selden to awaken to his love for her. Immediately following this display Lily and Selden escape to the garden, which has the feeling of an extension of Lily's tableau vivante. It is in this "magic place" that their "dream-like sensations" continued to flow through them (108). However, for Lily this is a false sense of union. She knows that the foundation upon which they were building their evening was not truly her, but an impersonation of another. That evening the sign she created for him in the picture did not inspire his imagination, only his fancy. She opens the conversation reminding Selden of the negative impression he has of her and of his failing to fulfill his promises earlier (108–109). She is, in effect, trying to snap him out of the romantic delusion of the tableau. She knows that in reality he will not be able to love her the way she desires despite his claim that he can only "help…by loving" her (109).

Considering that up to this point his help has been incomplete, so must his love for her be as unfulfilling as the woman thought her husband's love was in "The Fullness of Life." Instead, she tells him that he can love her, but she does not want to know about his love because she realizes that it is only his fancy speaking to her in a faux Republic. He had ignored her earlier cries to take her beyond while they were in the "finer air" of Bellomont (59). Only in this faux place, brought about by Lily becoming another and appealing to Selden's romantic fantasies, that he is willing to love her. She has to use the faux Republic because she cannot openly express her desire for him. He had ignored her earlier appeal at Bellomont when Lily desperately seeking a deeper union with him. By becoming his unchangeable ideal she makes him realize that she really does need his help. He was able to ignore it earlier because she had not fully been able to reach his imagination. Although her tableau tickles his fancy, there is the hope that it will inspire his imagination as well. She hopes that this will allow him to see her as his equal, not a dependent.

As long as the spell of the romanticized Lily intoxicates him, he is able to maintain the aura of loving her. The next morning she receives a note from him requesting a meeting, but she knows that his sending it is a result of acting out of the afterglow of her created death from the night before (110). In other words, she thinks he really does not mean his intentions and it is just a reaction to the spectacle she put on the previous night when he thought she touched him. Although she intends to deny his request, when it comes time to respond, she is unable to refuse. In part, this inability is because she hopes that he is willing to take the next step to give her the spiritual union she desires.

Selden is able to bask in the glow of his feelings for Lily as long as the living Lily does not physically intrude on the image he created of her. Finally

Selden wonders if there is a deeper love within his reach than the trivial experiments he has participated in because now "he could vividly conceive of a love which should broaden and deepen till it became the central fact of life" (121). Once again, Lily has touched Selden in a way he had never contemplated by revealing another letter of the sign of the Republic to him. He finally sees a love and a life beyond the physical, erotic or sentimental experiments. He becomes open to the spiritual soul-love Lily desires. At this point, he begins to envision that the sentimental experiment is for the living, for those who become slaves to Eros, but he is finally able to imagine something more. He wants a love that is the spiritual union. Only after seeing Lily static and idealized does he realize that she is the woman with whom he can find this sort of love, that she is worthy of his soul. The picture he was able to create regarding Lily after seeing the tableau will enable him to see beyond the negatives everyone else is saying about her. This realization that she could be someone who can offer him a love beyond the sentimental experiment produces in him a desire to "take her beyond—beyond the ugliness, the pettiness, the attrition and corrosion of the soul—" (122). He finally sees that his role is to save her, to help her, to have the strength to pull them from the society that is harmful. He must take her beyond the material unions found on earth to the spiritual communion beyond the trivial and the physical.

He even believes that he has the strength to do this task. In fact, her weakness makes him think that he is stronger (125). In vampiric fashion, he is feeding off of her weakness in order to keep her weak and death-like while telling himself that he is working to save them both. He thinks of her as "at once the dead weight at his breast and the spar which should float them to safety" (125–126). She is at once both the dead and the passive living being which needs to be saved and needs to save another. Even his analogy comparing Lily to Andromeda when he contemplates saving her has Lily in a death-like position. The story of Perseus's love for Andromeda however is far from death-like. Theirs is a romantic love story, one of love at first sight (Grant 346). Perseus first sees her chained to the rocks as a sacrificial victim for her mother's bragging about Andromeda's beauty, thus angering the Nereids. Believing that she should be bound by "love-knots" instead of chains, Perseus offers to save her if he could have her as his wife in return (Ovid 103). Although her parents, King Cepheus and Queen Cassiope, offered their kingdom as a dowry, Perseus refused, only wanting the beautiful Andromeda as his reward. In aligning himself with Perseus, Selden is admitting his love for Lily's beauty and rejecting any material claims upon her. However, Selden's version of Lily as Andromeda is not of rescuing the beautiful girl and living happily with his reward. In fact, he infuses his description of the rescue with negative terms. He visualizes an Andromeda who "cannot rise and walk, but clings to [Perseus] with dragging arms as he beats back to land with his burden" (125). This image of the death-like Andromeda makes her a passive being, waiting for her rescuer and still being a burden, even after her rescue. It is even questionable why one would even want to save such an Andromeda. However, for Selden her limp posture and passive role make her the ideal, unchangeable woman. She becomes his ideal and is unchangeable since she is death-like. She cannot protest the image he has created for her. She will always need him to create her identity as long as she is in this state.

However, when he actually sees Lily living, living a life where she can make choices and act upon them, he falls from the heights of the Republic. His earlier comments that he will rescue her from the vicious attitudes and beliefs fade into the background. Considering he already knew what was said about Lily and the picture she imitated could have been of a woman of questionable reputation, the only thing that has changed for Selden is that he can no longer envision Lily as dead. The very act of making choices, for better or for worse, is a life-affirming action. He cannot pretend she is the limp Andromeda needing to be rescued. This knowledge causes him to avoid Lily, to pretend she does not exist. Upon becoming alive again, Lily becomes just another sentimental experiment.

Yet, when they enter the same social circle in Monte Carlo his feelings for her return because her beauty has suffered and appeared to be making her look as if her youthful beauty was dead (149). He maintains the vision of her as frozen, or partly dead, in order to justify his feelings for her and his need to rescue her. However, at the dinner table, when once again she is acting on her own and defying the role of the dead woman, he dislikes her again. In fact, he believes that her ability to make choices he thinks are detrimental caused him to be separated from her (168). His love for her did not stop because of the vulgar positions she found herself in, but because she made the choice to act on her own, to be an active agent, to be alive.

From this point on Selden physically removes himself as much as possible from Lily's life until her final visit. Her goal was to attempt to reach an understanding with him, yet he is not willing to meet her in that act (237). He elects to remain firmly planted in the physical, earthly realm and refuses to think of the life they could have beyond the physical. Lily thinks she will never regain access to Selden's soul because of this. (239). She knows that he has closed off the imaginative side of his self, although she is not quite sure why. Because she is not willing to relinquish her ideal easily, Lily attempts one final appeal to his soul by reminding him about their talk of the Republic at Bellomont which meant so much to her, but he still remains guarded. For Selden, however, it is not until he sees her bending before the fire that he realized "how thin her hands looked…how the curves of her figure had shrunk to angularity…how the red play of the flame sharpened the depression[s]…and intensified the blackness of the shadows" on her face that he is able to regain his love for her (241). It is when she seems thin, skeletal, and, in essence, deathlike that he is able to realize how much he cares for her.

Before she leaves, Lily realizes that "something in truth lay dead between them—the love she had killed in him and could no longer call to life. But something lived between them also, and leaped up in her like an imperishable flame: it was the love his love had kindled, the passion of her soul for his" (241). In an interesting change of roles, Lily finally sees that something is dead, but it is the erotic love that she inspired in him. He refuses to be a slave to Eros for her and, therefore, is no longer interested in her as a sentimental experiment. Unfortunately, he refuses to let himself see the other possibilities for their love. Lily, however, can see more. She is able to feel the communion of spirit that exists between them even if he is not willing or able to feel it at that moment. She realizes that although the potential material union between them is dead, they can love each other in spirit. The love that her soul feels for him is the offspring of their relationship. The two of them, perhaps semi-unwittingly, have given birth to a love beyond the physical. It is this offspring, in the imagined form of Nettie's baby, which Lily holds on to at her death. It is the love of her soul for his that allows them, finally, to "speak" to each other beyond.

The next day, after her true physical death, Selden finds that he is finally able to embrace an emotional connection in his pursuit of Lily (252). He has finally decided to pursue the spiritual union with the woman he had been thinking of as a sentimental experiment. Yet, when he finds her dead, he feels distanced from her physical beauty (253). The shock at finding her really dead eventually gives way to Selden being able to see "deep into the hidden things of love" (253). Without the dead Lily, he never would have come to this realization. He now knows what it means to find a spiritual union, but the unfortunate part is that he can only find this meaning in a dead woman's body. As Helen Killoran writes, Selden realizes that "a true 'republic of the spirit,' freedom from materialism, exists only in the republic of the grave" (26).

He does realize, while looking over the dead body, that "it was this moment of love, this fleeting victory over themselves, which had kept them from atrophy and extinction; which, in her, had reached out to him in every struggle against the influence of her surroundings, and in him, had kept alive the faith that now drew him penitent and reconciled to her side" (256). It is in her death that Selden finally realizes that Lily was reaching out to him while alive. He realizes that, with his help, she could have overcome her surroundings to enter into the Republic of the Spirit together. He finally has the faith in their love. However, it is only at her death that he can realize this. He is reconciled to the mockery he made of both of their lives by denying the spiritual communion that she tried to reach with him. Yet, her death also forces an awakening in him, just as she had awakened him in the earlier tableau scene.

While in his silent and penitent state, "there passed between them the word which made all clear" (256). As to be expected, when words are not mentioned, there are numerous suggestions for what that word could be which passed between them. The usual readings see the word as "love" or "faith" (Joslin, *Wharton* 67). Considering the true spiritual soul-love that Lily seeks can only be found beyond life, it only makes sense for the word which passes between them to be the word which comes to mean the most to both of them: "beyond" (Joslin, *Wharton* 68). Not only is this the word which appears on Lily's calling card, but it is also the word which Selden clings to the first time he thinks he is in love with her. Also, it represents where the love they both seek, a love that is more than just a material love, can take place: beyond the real world in the afterlife.

It is only during her death or death-like states that Selden can find the clues to his love for Lily. When she is alive and beautiful, he is most often offended by her actions and her actual living. This is because the kind of love they both seek can only be found in the spiritual union ultimately revealed when Lily dies. Interestingly, the death of one of the characters, allows for union of feeling for both. Finally, Selden is able to see the real Lily. Selden will no longer change his feelings for Lily because she cannot act to make him dislike her. Her feelings for him will not change, because she has finally reached a static state in death.

True understanding about love can only happen when one of the intended mates is dead. It appears, at this point in her works, that Wharton believes that real love, that true love, that true spiritual unions can only occur in death. What is left on earth is a Darwinian parody of true love expressed through in material unions. Through the juxtaposing of Darwin's notion of sexual selection and Plato's notion of love, "Wharton clearly condemns a social system that separates eros and love" (Honey 82). Since society honors material relationships and Wharton does not portray that society in the best light, the material relationships cannot be the ideal love relationship for Wharton and her characters. Thus, in *The House of Mirth*, Wharton presents us with the image that the ideal love relationship is the spiritual communion in the Republic of the Spirit, but it is found only in death. This tension between ideal love and physical love continues in *The Fruit of the Tree*. However, Wharton furthers the conflict by showing the effect on a living mate as well as a dead mate.

CHAPTER FOUR
The Fruit of the Tree

With her next novel, *The Fruit of the Tree*, Wharton begins to revise her concept of the Republic of the Spirit in relation to the conflict between spiritual love and physical love. She no longer refers to the ideal world beyond the physical as the Republic of the Spirit, but begins to place the true love of one soul for another in the "inner kingdom" that the person creates for themselves, but that a like mind would understand (Wharton, *Fruit* 152). One finds many of the same elements of the Republic appear in the inner kingdom such as building their love upon friendship, a feeling of a greater understanding between the two souls and the physical descriptions that Lily and Selden find at Bellomont. However, in *The Fruit of the Tree*, Amherst has to pass through the spell of physical love in the faux Republic before finding what he believes is a balanced love.

For many critics, the primary fault with novel is that it is beyond Wharton's world. In selecting to write this novel of industrial reform, Wharton, stepped beyond her abilities, covered too many topics or did not have the confidence needed to write successfully (Lewis 181; Wershoven 124; Wolff, *Feast* 135). Katherine Joslin, however, in her analysis of the novel's design, views Justine's story as the novel's center, not the story of the Mills ("Architectonic" 72). Given that Wharton was reading Plato's *Phaedrus* and *Symposium* while writing *Fruit* it could be that Wharton planned to tell the conflict between an ideal spiritual love and physical love through Justine's roles in fixing and creating romantic relationships. When we look beyond the surface text of the struggles of a mill owner for reform and focus instead upon the interaction between love and death the story becomes one of a man and a woman struggling to find their ideal soul love in a world governed by Darwinian sexual selection.

It is the conflict between platonic thought and Darwinian sexual selection which illuminates the relationships between the characters. Justine's free thinking makes her one of Plato's "non-lovers" who seek a soul love and philosophic wisdom. She shares Amherst's ideals and encourages him to new heights of wisdom. Bessy, on the other hand, represents the Darwin's theory in action in that she is a perfect mate according to sexual selection. She is a physically attractive woman who seeks the marriage bond solely as a connection of bodies (323). She is the one who has the traits which enable her to select her mate based on Darwin's theory. In her role of the physical lover, she "awakens" Amherst's sexual and monetary desires (Papke 125).

Despite the immediate mental union between Justine and Amherst, he cannot or will not acknowledge his feelings for her until death has impacted her life. Bessy, the physical lover, has already been touched by death and therefore is more beautiful because of it. Her hold on Amherst, her beauty, is immediately linked to death because she is the widow of the former mill owner. When she first arrives at the Hopewood, Amherst and Justine do not notice her striking beauty, but that her veil shadowed her "fair pale face" (20). He cannot even remember her name, only that she is the widow of the former mill owner. Amherst, from their first meeting, believes that Bessy *is* the mills. By equating the woman with the lifeless land, Amherst reinforces the notion that she is also one of the living dead, just like the mill. She does not have an identity of her own; she is only seen in terms of her grief for her former husband. As a recent widow, she has been touched by death in the most explicit way short of her own death. Not only did she lose her husband, but, it can be argued, that she would have been seen as losing part of herself since in marriage the two are made one. She becomes a walking symbol of her husband's death and the dying mills.

Amherst's position in relation to his romantic choices for mates presents an interesting contrast to Selden's. With Selden, Wharton had depicted a man on the outer orbit of society being pursued by a woman entrenched in the physical, Bertha, and one who prefers a spiritual union, Lily. Because the physical realm influenced Selden more than he was willing to acknowledge, he was unable to have a complete union with Lily until her death when all he was left with was the physical body in the real world. Although Amherst's situation and choices seem very similar to Selden's (the physical is primary in Bessy's life as it was with Bertha and the spiritual is primary in Justine's life as it was with Lily), Amherst is only interested in how he can use the physical to help others. As if to emphasize his early lack of interest in the physical, he had rejected wealth in his youth for his ideals, rejected the physical for the imagination. In theory, all the obstacles Selden faced in reaching the physical and spiritual union with Lily have been removed from Amherst's path. One would even think that with Amherst's removal from the physical, he would be more open to an ideal union of souls.

Although death surrounds Justine and Amherst's first meeting, she takes such a clinical view of death in order to emphasize that it has not touched her personally. Her professional instinct overrules any touch that death could have on her (15). They first meet in the surgical ward surrounded by an aura of death. Here they are able to take the first steps in creating their spiritual union of like ideals. While discussing an earlier death in the ward they realize that they had a similar sense of humor (12). Their bond is immediate and deep, rooted in their views. Not only do they share the same view on Dillon's case and on the state of Westmore's mills, but they also refuse to acknowledge their feelings for each other until much later, after death has touched them both personally. Interestingly, it is the thought of Justine that prompts Amherst to begin to imagine the perfect woman. His ideal is "the woman who kept a calm exterior . . ." but also in whom "the springs of feeling lay close to the unruffled surface" (27). At the time of their first meeting, Amherst believes that Justine has the first part, but he is unable to ascertain how deep her emotions run. In fact, he does not even try. She is available for a spiritual union, but he does not realize how passionate she can be. This is strange, considering their immediate bond and the signs of his attachment for her.

Amherst does, however, show outward physical signs of an emotional attachment for Justine. When thinking about her and her actions, he looked different (27), and he regretted that he had missed seeing her during her visit to the mill (71). Yet, by the time they reunite, Bessy Westmore's physical attractiveness already has him in its web. Bessy is able to take him away from Justine because of her physical beauty and her being a stronger, surviving mate from a previous relationship. The distraction is so complete that Amherst is willing to sacrifice the deeper union he can have with Justine for the physically desirable Bessy. Desire and lust overrule the soul for Amherst. It appears that Plato's warning that this desire and lust can corrupt the soul seeking spiritual beauty will come to fruition (*Phaedrus* 34).

In contrast with his meeting with Justine, his early interactions with Bessy strike him silent. He was left speechless at the sight of her beauty, thus unable to discover her nature or her opinions (49). Although his mind was rushing to find a common ground for a deeper union with Bessy, it is not available to him because her physical desirability is so overwhelming and consuming. He will never get beyond her physical love to a deeper spiritual love with her. There is not the easy interaction of soul mates finding each other, but the interaction of a man dumbfounded by the potential of a physical relationship with a physically attractive mate. Bessy's physical beauty, in conjunction with her flirtatious interest in Amherst, serves to pull him away from the intellectual bond he has with Justine. And Bessy, as depicted by her interactions with Amherst, is truly a flirt; she feigns interest in the mills just to entice him. It appears that only Amherst is blind to Bessy's manipulative charms. While he believes she is truly interested in his ideas, others see that she is just accommodating him until she wins his love. Even the mill employees distrust her interest at her visit as seen in their faces and their coldness toward her (61). Although Amherst sees their discomfort, it does not fit into his view of Bessy so he creates an elaborate fantasy to explain their response and emphasizes his belief in her beauty.

In order to keep his fantasy of her potential intellectual beauty, Amherst must misread her actions as a sign of her willingness to let him educate her into his realm of ideals. To do this, he imagines her summoning him regarding the mills and submitting to his way of thinking (100). For Bessy, however, this submission has nothing to do with being educated or united in an ideal, but a desire to satisfy her physical urges for Amherst. He has yet to realize that Bessy's mind had never been awoken to Amherst's world or any potential deeper union or kingdom. Instead, she focused on and desired physical things (259). Bessy, it seems lacks the imagination not only to find the inner kingdom, but also to conceive of it. Considering that Wharton has now placed the soul union in the inner kingdom of the lover, Bessy will forever be inadequately prepared for reaching it. In fact, her lack of mental prowess is mentioned throughout the novel. She cannot see the importance of issues that he brings to her attention. Amherst believes she is like his mother whose mind was only able to comprehend the physical (119). Yet, there is nothing concrete about the inner kingdom that Bessy would be able to hold on to for a deeper union. Instead, she would rather be "interesting" rather than to live with an interesting man (226). She believes that men are only devoted to interesting women, not intellectual ones.

Amherst, not initiated in the ways of the coquette, confuses her charms with the qualities he is seeking in a mate. He even feels that she has the qualities that he is looking for in a woman; she has a calm exterior in emergencies and, as Mrs. Ansell points out, deeper passions (88). Yet, because her calm exterior is truly a reflection of her lack of concern, her focus goes no further than fulfilling her own desires. Mrs. Ansell recognizes that Bessy's interest in Amherst stems from neither love nor desire to improve the mills, but from boredom (89). Her family would prefer that she take a hobby, any hobby, to deter her from her flirtatious interest in Amherst. They do not fear that he will form a deeper soul union with her, but that he will separate her from her money. In fact, they do not even begin to consider that there could be a happy union between Amherst and Bessy. Instead, they see that Amherst provides the extra enticement of bringing about the passion that she never experienced in her first marriage (89). When Langhope cannot understand this desire for excitement, Mrs. Ansell must explain it to him. She believes that "Bessy wasn't awake, she wasn't even born" during her first marriage (90). Bessy is conscious only after the death of her first husband. Now that this has happened, the questions become: to what or whom does she awaken? In *The House of Mirth* and "The Fullness of Life," as we have seen, death awakens the surviving person to recognize love, yet that Bessy's awakening is a more destructive force. Mrs. Ansell believes that Bessy, upon this awakening, will be seeking pleasure through impulsive actions. Although it seems as though she is heading in the direction of destroying Amherst or his ideals, her desire is not to inflict harm. Instead of moving toward a fuller spiritual love, Bessy is moving toward acknowledging the physical nature of her desires. In other words, she is more open to a physical grand passion than a spiritual union because she is a slave to her impulses.

In an interesting juxtaposition, the scene in which Mrs. Ansell tells Langhope of Bessy's awakening is immediately followed by the scene of Amherst contemplating the depth of his blindness to the world around him. He was so oblivious to the nature of the female that his interactions with Bessy were completely unexpected (91). He was not anticipating her to awaken his physical desire at the expense of his spiritual ideals. In fact, he had spent his life up to this point shying away from female contact and his physical nature (91). In the past, he had been so preoccupied with the ideal side that there was no room for a physical love. Bessy's powerful physical beauty changes that. His imagination had wholly been preoccupied with higher concerns and he falls under "the ancient spell" of her beauty (91). In selecting Amherst, Bessy selects a mate who is still asleep to the ways of the world. She brings him under the "spell" of the faux Republic. While her primitive side had been awakened at the end of her first marriage, his primitive side is just beginning to awaken under her influence. He still tries to hold on to the ideal by writing a new history for Bessy, thus creating his ideal woman and ignoring Bessy's true self.

Bessy's lack of interest in the larger questions of life becomes explicit when visiting Dillon in the hospital. After the visit, Amherst notices that Bessy's interest was only as it applied to her, not that of a larger interest in the safety of the mill employees (104). It is obvious that Bessy is not suited for the higher elements Amherst desires of her. Amherst, however, becomes overtaken by her beauty so much so that he forgets his original concerns regarding her ability to see beyond herself (105). In other words, her physical beauty overwhelms her intellectual deficiencies. She is not the full-fledged soul mate for Amherst. She is only one small part of his ideal and her beauty is purely physical.

Given Amherst's preoccupation with Bessy's beauty, one would tend to think that Justine was not beautiful. However, Wharton makes it explicitly clear that Justine is beautiful, but Amherst is blind to it until much later in the story. Everything about her is spirit and life (143). She looks young and is compared to the heart of a rose (145). Perhaps Amherst is blind to Justine's beauty because he believes she is more closely aligned with the spiritual realm than the physical realm. Even in her work, her imagination would help her deal with the pain and suffering surrounding her (144). Even though bodies and physically ill people surround her, she appears to be untouched by physical concerns. Instead, her imagination shows her that it is the spirit of the patients that matters most. In fact, the extreme physical nature of her work is what she wishes to quell. Because they share similar ideals, Amherst's fear of a spiritual union with his ideal soul mate is what blinds him to Justine's beauty. In order to reinforce that Justine is beautiful, some of the other men in the novel attempt to corrupt Justine's desire for a spiritual union by bringing her into the physical love governed by sexual selection. Westy Gaines consistently tries to impress her with his social standing because he finds her so beautiful. He appeals to her based on his wallet and his physical desirability to other women, but Justine will not participate in the battle for his attentions.

Justine's other suitor, Dr. Stephen Wyant, appears to be a perfect match for her. He should understand her work and is physically attractive. Even Justine feels they have similar interests and feelings (240). However, that disappears when he is physically present. When he is absent, she can create an ideal version of him as the one man who would understand her physical desires. She is looking for a man in whom she can create and express her ideal. Only her idealized mate would have the soul needed to penetrate her ideal realm. While he is gone, she is able to create her version of Wyant, but it is only in his presence that his preoccupation with the physical becomes apparent. Although this makes him a superior doctor, it also allows him to fall victim to drugs to dull the pain. Wyant, however, sees Justine as the perfect helpmate for him in work and in physical love, but Justine wants more out of love and marriage than what Wyant offers (369).

Although it seems obvious that marriage to Amherst would be a marriage in which "two colours blend, two textures are the same," Amherst, at this point in his life, is too fascinated by Bessy's beauty to consider Justine as a mate (369). He is still infatuated with Bessy and the desire that her physical beauty would be mirrored by an equally beautiful soul (108). Although her face and spirit may complete each other, they do not do so in the way Amherst desires. Bessy's concern for the mills goes no further than her physical attraction to Amherst. Her concern, just like her beauty, is superficial.

During the final stages of his courtship of Westmore's widow, Amherst believes that she has begun to awaken to a spiritual union with him (120). He did start her thinking about improvements, but not in the way he planned. In fact, her actual thoughts had never occurred to him. Instead of improving the mill for others, Bessy's concerns are to make the mill better for her own physical improvement. Occasionally, Amherst does have moments of clarity regarding Bessy's lack of ability to join him in a higher love, but those are only when she is not physically present. He begins to feel that her intuition and instinct will never be what he desires them to be (125). In other words, once she has removed the spell of her physical beauty, he begins to distrust Bessy's ability to become his ideal intellectual mate. He leaves her faux kingdom for a return to his ideals. Although, she is still a physical beauty and he admires her heart, her intellect is sorely lacking. Amherst would never be able to reach the deeper union with her that he could reach with Justine.

Amherst does attempt to draw Bessy into the heights of a union of souls through a physical approximation of the feelings they would have in a deeper union. The description of their sled ride parallels the description of Lily and Selden's feelings discussing the Republic of the Spirit in *The House of Mirth*. The thrill of the speed of the sled, combined with the potential of death and injury filled Amherst "with a strange intensity of life" (132–133). It is interesting to note, that although this sled ride fills Bessy and Amherst with a feeling of truly being alive another sled ride, which appears in *Ethan Frome*, acts to destroy all life for the woman involved. As Bessy and Amherst plunge toward the bottom of the hill, however, he felt "as though his body had been left behind, and only the spirit in him rode the…air . . ." (133–134). This is a feeling which he thought Bessy shared with him (134). For Amherst, the movement from body to spirit not only brings them closer to the ideal union of mind and body, but also enables them to enter the "enchanted forest" (135). Yet, the spell does not last long for Bessy as she is moved by impulse to seek a new thrill (134). For her, the excitement was not in feeling the thrill of a deeper union, but the thrill of the impulsive nature of the event.

As her impulse leads him to this forest, his feelings begin to cool (135). Once led away from possible death, Amherst's "sensations were not of that highest order of happiness where mind and heart mingle their elements in the strong draught of life," (135–136). In other words, this is a charmed union, not an ideal spiritual union because it was created while under the spell of the physical. The fact that this is not the spiritual union is further enhanced by Amherst's discovery that they had not penetrated very deep into their physical or spiritual surroundings. Bessy's impulses can lead him into an approximation of the deep penetrating view of her soul, but in reality, they can only barely scratch the surface. Her flights of fancy are just an expression of her needing constant physical entertainment and nothing deeper (371). Because of this, the concept of the enchanted forest seems to represent a faux inner kingdom, just as the garden scene in *The House of Mirth* represented a faux Republic of the Spirit. It is a charmed version of the kingdom, not the true kingdom. This venture will characterize Amherst's and Bessy's marriage. Their physical attraction remains, but a deeper union of like thoughts and souls will never be theirs because she lacks the imagination for anything more.

After Amherst's marriage, Justine and Bessy start changing places regarding life, love and death. Justine is awakened to death, so much so that she feels that there was something inherently wrong with being so young and having "to live in perpetual contact with decay and pain—to look persistently into the grey face of death without having lifted even a corner of life's veil" (147). Interestingly, as we shall see later this notion of the veil will return again in *Twilight Sleep*, where Pauline is seeking a mentor to take her "beyond the veil" of life (273). In Justine's case, however, she is surrounded by death, but feels that she has not even lived yet. She feels the dread of a direct connection to death as opposed to earlier where she was able to ignore the physical realities. Being touched by death allows Justine to voice her view of love.

Justine's believes that there is someone for her who can awaken "the wings under the skin, that sprout when one meets a...kindred" pair (148). It is in *Phaedrus*, perhaps, where this tale has its roots. There Socrates explains that the "philosophic way of life" in love will allow the participants to "have full-grown wings and cast off the burdens of the flesh" (Plato, *Phaedrus* 41). The friendship that lovers form allows for their "journey of radiant happiness together, and when they grow their wings, these shall be alike because of their love" once they leave their bodies (Plato, *Phaedrus* 41–42). This kind of love is only found when two kindred souls live a philosophic life. Justine hopes for the kind of love that will provide her with those shoulders to help her find her wings. In other words, she hopes to find her true soul mate who can find his way to her "secret precinct" (152). Once she begins to think about her love taking wing, she wonders if Amherst is experiencing a similar growth with Bessy. Much like Selden, Justine created her own version of the Republic of the Spirit that she hopes to enter with her soul mate. Her secret place was a world she

> had created for herself, an inner kingdom where the fastidiousness she had to set aside in her outward relations recovered its full sway. There must be actual beings worthy of admission to this secret precinct, but hitherto they had not come her way; and the sense that they were somewhere just out of reach still gave an edge of youthful curiosity to each encounter (152).

Justine's inner world is a place where the mind and soul take precedence over physical desires. She knows in this place she will be able to maintain an outer shell of calmness and also have share deeper feelings with another just as Amherst desires in his mate. It is not a place for her to inhabit alone, though, but a place for her and her kindred spirit. Thus, much like Lily Bart in *The House of Mirth*, she is aware of a greater world where she and an allied spirit could live. The challenge is trying to unite with that spirit so they could find and cross the threshold to enter the ideal realm together.

Bessy's influence on Amherst threatens to make him an unacceptable inhabitant in Justine's kingdom. The fact that he has seemingly given up the ideals they had formerly shared makes Justine think he would prefer Bessy's physical love to Justine's spiritual love. Amherst's experiences with Bessy, however, have left him completely disillusioned with physical love. He no longer believes that he could help Bessy reach the higher passions, and he has relinquished all hope that she complements his high ideals with her presence. In fact, he had begun to relinquish the delusion that the best women followed the poet's verse that "*He for God only, she for God in him.* It was for the god in him, surely, that she had loved him: for that first glimpse of an 'ampler ether, a diviner air' that he" revealed to her (179–180). The poet in question is, of course, John Milton and this line comes from the section detailing Adam and Eve in the Garden of Eden in Book 4 of *Paradise Lost*. Although they both resemble their maker, the passage breaks down their essences into Adam being the intellectual one and Eve being the graceful one (4:297–298). Although Eve exists "for God in him" (4:299), Book 8 of *Paradise Lost* shows that she is also capable of the same level of intelligence that Adam is. It is just that Eve prefers Adam educating her since he:

> she knew would intermix
> Grateful digressions, and solve high dispute
> With conjugal Caresses, from his Lip
> Not Words alone pleas'd her (8:54–57).

In other words, Eve enjoyed loving kisses along with her discussions. It is also interesting to note that this builds upon the notion of a perfect union, joining the Platonic separation of body and mind. It would seem that this is the perfect situation, but when Bessy does not see Amherst as the ultimate vessel of God, the parallel falls short and they do not achieve his desires for a complete physical and spiritual union. He never once thought that she could have ideals of her own for them both, but assumes that she should want everything he wants. This assumption is easy for him to make because he never saw her as she truly was. Instead, he saw her as an idealized physical beauty to love and mold into his image of the ideal woman to love. In attempting to write her history, he fails to take into account that she is a living woman instead of a dead body. As a living woman, her actions take away his ability to create a new identity for her and refuse to permit him to gain his self-worth through her.

In marrying Amherst, Bessy takes one step away from the realm of death into the realm of an active life. The marriage allows her to relinquish the identity of the widow, the dead body, and become the wife again, become alive. This new classification moves her from the dead mourner to the living helpmate. As this change happens, Amherst begins to see how he misjudged his wife's potential spiritual union with him (183). His life, he fears, will become completely dominated by the physical at the sake of higher thoughts and feelings (185). Finally, the appeal of Bessy's physical beauty is not enough to keep Amherst and Bessy together. The spell is broken when he learns that she rejects his idealized view of her, in effect rejecting his desire for her to have faith in him. In a significant way, the Amhersts's views of the mills are also their views toward their relationship. For Bessy, the Mill's spirit could be free only if she retained control of "its body" (202). This is how she views Amherst. He can have his grand ideas as long as they remain in the confines of the law of her physical desires. By forcing Bessy to conform to his ideals, Amherst is not conforming to her physical needs. He, however, desires to see the body and spirit of the mills united in one being: Bessy Westmore, thus turning Bessy into the ultimate symbol.

Amherst quickly discovers that Bessy's soul was concerned with "the immediate pleasure" and that "she had not enough imagination to look beyond" (204). The immediate pleasure is key to Bessy's personality. Her imagination cannot conceive of the realm beyond. Since these are two prerequisites to the Republic, Bessy will never be able to unlock the door to a greater union. She gives her body to the immediate, impulsive pleasure, not to the deeper union of the soul. The men in her life believe she is incapable of knowing the higher pleasures of the soul and lacks the imagination found in Justine to create a realm of the inner world. It is only when Amherst points out that Bessy has rendered him impotent with her actions regarding the mill that she is willing to acquiesce to his point of view. Bessy's acquiescence, however, is a hollow victory for Amherst. It serves to make him powerfully aware of his wife's inability to conceive of a higher realm and, in the process, she unknowingly emasculated him. Since she cannot see beyond the personal impulse, she was not aware that her actions would have the effect upon Amherst that they did. He elects to run from the meetings, rather than be unable to function as a strong man without his wife's permission (205).

As Bessy moves further away from the death she embraced when Amherst was courting her, Justine moves closer to death. She finds life at Lynbrook to be filled with "deadening influences" which forced her to fight back "as a suffocated person" would fight against death (222). This image recurs throughout Wharton's works. Once Justine is living in a world of death, a world where Bessy and those like Bessy find life, she begins to feel the call of romance. Much like Amherst, Justine wishes for a better life where she and her mate can meet on the level of kindred souls (223). The joining of usefulness and enjoyment is something foreign to Bessy, but innate to those who see the higher purpose of life.

The physical separation allows Amherst to realize that he no longer feels for Bessy as he once did (247). Although passion, based upon physical beauty and lust, still remains, the deeper feelings of sentiment are gone, if they ever did exist outside of Amherst's idealized world. There is no stronger bond between them than physical attraction for each other to keep them together and upon which to build a deeper understanding. While Amherst and Bessy are growing further apart, Amherst and Justine find themselves growing closer together. She becomes his confidante and he trusts her implicitly, as she trusts him. While Bessy and Amherst seek a faithful devotion from each other, Justine and Amherst seek honest communication (253).

The lack of a common, unifying language further divides Amherst and Bessy from each other in that they cannot communication on the same level. He discovers that Bessy and her surroundings "spoke a language so different" that he felt it impossible to make her want to understand him (249). Yet, this is not the case with his relationship with Justine. In fact, Justine's language provides Amherst with a sense of complete understanding and empathy which is lacking in his marriage (255). Justine provides that union of truth, compassion and understanding that can be found in united souls. She, not Bessy, seems to be the better mate for Amherst. Even the most basic necessities which could help bring a couple closer together are removed from their life, thus making it impossible for them to bond even on the most primitive level of basic needs (296). The only thing left is his admiration of her beauty.

It is important to note, however, that Amherst is not the only one suffering for his choice. Bessy, in her changed role of living wife, believes that Amherst did not love her as he should have since he "disturbed the foundations of her world" without thinking of the consequences to her (264). She does not understand that he was trying to bring her into the ideal realm beyond. Because of this lack of insight, Bessy begins to hate him for making her a live woman again, instead of letting her remain the "dead" widow (264). She was not capable of being a living, thinking, analytical being; she was made for impulse and it is impulse that will eventually return her to the idealized dead.

Yet, her beauty still had a powerful effect upon him, provoking his lust to the extreme. To Amherst, no matter how bad their relationship becomes, she is always the woman who awakened him to physical beauty and desires (267). Although Bessy's beauty roused him, marrying her forced him to try to close his mind to the ideas upon which he thrived. If he were as dead to the concept of a deeper union as she was, they would have been blissful in their physical relationship. That, however, is not the case and, although her beauty will never have the same effect upon him, he still felt sympathy for her (267). He has lost interest in the full union with her while she is the living embodiment of his wife. She no longer is the idealized, idolized woman. Only after her death will she regain this prominence in his life; only after she has returned to the dead state which first attracted him, will he love her again.

It is just at the moment when Bessy and Amherst are farthest apart, when "the last of these veils had been torn away" (298), that Amherst and Justine enter into the inner realm in the "aromatic essences embalming a dead summer" (299). This dead summer echoes the lingering summer found when Lily and Selden discuss the Republic in *The House of Mirth* and will reappear in later works. With Justine in the lead, guiding them not only deeper into the forest, but also deeper into her soul, they reach their ideal moment of deeper understanding and communion. Interestingly, this moment where "one never says, *This is the moment!* Because, however good it is, it always seems the door to a better one beyond," recalls the beyond of Lily

Bart's Republic (304). Traveling beyond, for Justine and Amherst is something that they see as a better future than the one they currently possess. This is what makes Lily's Republic unattainable while alive, but gives Justine's inner realm the hope of being actualized. It is in this aura of dead summer that Amherst is able to rekindle the feeling of boyishness that he had felt on the sled before his marriage. His rejuvenation kindles a similar feeling in Justine. This youthful feeling in the presence of death brings their souls together in an ideal realm. There they feel the equivalent to the "long flight" of a bird that is able to remain happiest in "the thick of everyday life" (304). The bird is able to fly, but will always return to her old life (303). The knowledge of her travels beyond is what she can live upon while being forced to stay in her mundane everyday existence. Cicely's appearance, a tiny image of her mother, terminates Amherst's flight in recalling his earlier flight and its consequences.

As Bessy becomes more alive, active and assertive, Amherst moves Justine closer to the center of his life. She becomes the united mind to which he holds himself accountable. She becomes the touchstone for reclaiming his ideals, yet it is also under Justine's influence that he is able to see that leaving Bessy would be a break with the physical past and a devastating destruction (339). This thought of Bessy suffering encourages him to give her lifestyle another try. However, he returns to find her snubbing him for her new life with the Carburys. In other words, just as he is thinking of her wounded and suffering, her reasserting her life and desires serves as a check on his ideals. He must admit that his idealized notion of Bessy suffering was just a fantasy, not the reality of her life.

Once Bessy breaks free of Amherst's shadow, she blossoms physically. Before the separation, she was always ailing and in need of Nurse Justine. After the break, Justine remarks that Bessy had never looked healthier (346). Bessy had never been more alive. In an attempt to maintain this life, she avoids time alone with Justine and the reminder of her husband that Justine evokes. However, once they are alone, Bessy feels the crippling, chocking force of Amherst. As their chat progresses, "her face lost the bloom of animation…and she looked so pale and weary…" as she touched the "chain about her neck" (348). Justine's appearance reminds her of Amherst, and the thought of having to conform to his ideal, an ideal for which she was not raised. The chain around her neck, a symbol of Amherst's marriage, begins to tighten and chafe her.

After her accident, Bessy must fight for her life both literally and figuratively. She is in a world where each day is a struggle for life in the face of death, but without the hope of a loving soul to save her. Even her house takes on the aura of sickness and death. Most disheartening for those surrounding her is the knowledge that if she does live, her life would no longer be a physical one, but a life of paralysis. She would be confined to a life of the mind and spirit, something that she would not even consider when alive. With Bessy begging for death and after reading Amherst's marginalia from one of his library books, a potential sign from Amherst, Justine elects to end the suffering (432). She acts to treat Bessy as Justine would want to be treated. Justine believes that Bessy's mind is suffering because Bessy's body is no longer able to sustain her physical desires. Her act to put an end to her friend's spiritual suffering is an act of kindness, reflecting the ideals she believes she shares with Amherst. It is their ideals taking physical form instead of remaining in the higher ether.

Justine's actions, converting the living Bessy to the dead woman, give Amherst the ability to create his ideal woman once again. Bessy can no longer fight to change the history Amherst desires to create for her. Instead, she must passively accept his idealized version of her. His wife has finally become his ideal dead woman, and Justine, his mental equal, has been touched not only by death, but also is the agent of death. His first impulse in idealizing Bessy is to believe that her leaving the mills to him is a sign of her faith in him and his ideals (437). Yet, given Bessy's feelings toward Amherst at the time of her death, it was, most likely, just another of her impulsive actions that she had not yet reversed.

Interestingly, Amherst's view of Justine suddenly changes after Bessy's death. She becomes, more completely, his ideal mate, body and soul. Although he still admires and desires to see her for her mind, he also awakens to her physical desirability and marriageability. He thinks that she has grown and matured to kindle these feelings of love in him (449). Yet, the only thing that had changed of late was that Justine became an agent of death. Having once been "tricked" by a woman's physical beauty, Amherst is not quick to put his faith in Justine's physical and mental union with him. However, she eventually becomes not only his desirable soul mate, but also a constant, living reminder of his wife's death. Although she now carries "the darkness of the world's pain in her eyes" (463), Amherst feels that she is more feminine and approachable than she had ever been to him (464). Bessy's death has transformed not only her, but also Justine.

Amherst's proposal to Justine is an appeal to the mind, not the body. In fact, he did not tell her she was beautiful, instead selecting to focus on the improvements to the mill they could make together (465). What he had to give was a life of philanthropy and stewardship based on like minds and ideals. Whereas Bessy and Amherst were wooed by each other's beauty, Justine and Amherst are wooed by each other's ideals. Justine, however, feels there is something more for them. She believes they can find happiness in a deeper union through marriage. She accepts his proposal because she believes she can reawaken his ideals and soul (471). She hopes to bring his secret self to her soul's world; she hopes he is worthy. His secret self had long been dead and buried by life with Bessy. It is this self, which appeals to Justine, which she hopes will help her with finding the higher purpose in the mundane world (471). The lovers have returned to where they began; only they have switched roles. Instead of Amherst awakening Bessy to the beauty of a spiritual union, Justine attempts to reawaken Amherst to the spiritual. Amherst has spent so much time in the unhappy realm of physical love that all he can offer her is a life of enacting their shared ideals.

Interestingly, for a while their life is purely wedded bliss. Although the shadow of Bessy's death hangs over their actions, they have the spiritual union to help them perform their mill reform in unison. Their life is a union of equals who are soul mates in mind and body in the shadow of death. However, Justine is afraid to look at their life too closely for fear of losing what they have due to her actions. Justine begins to think their happiness is not real and maintainable (490). As soon as she reveals her part in Bessy's death, she realizes how shaky their happiness is. Their mental union breaks as he expresses his shock and horror. The complete understanding that they had previously possessed is ruined. Justine's actions force the couple to eat from the tree of knowledge and deal with the consequences. Although she felt that he was her life's center, all he can see is that Justine acted alone to kill his now idealized Bessy (525). He only saw her actions, actions which proclaimed her life, her free will, and forced them to question their intellectual union. This lack of understanding forced Justine to believe that they could never return to the comfortable harmony they had before (527). She does not blame herself for this break, but blames his lack of faith in her and their ideals.

In order to save what is left of their life and their deeper union, Justine leaves, effectively becoming dead to Amherst, to save him. Her departing demonstrates that she has a greater knowledge of how his mind functions than he does. In leaving him, she hopes he will eventually be able to return to her and they can rekindle their past through his being able to create an idealized version of her in his imagination. Her absence will allow him the freedom to rediscover the ideals he had once found in her. What Justine does not account for is that her actions force Amherst to rethink his idea of womanhood (560). Instead of seeing women being ruled by physical desires and impulse, as Bessy was, he needs to accommodate for a woman controlled by the mind. He has to admit that the woman he loves is not an ideal but a real woman. Although she was capable of higher, spiritual impulses, she is also subject to the physical impulses they both feel. He can no longer see her as an ideal or as physical impulse alone, but as his intellectual equal. Yet, he still sees the man as lord over his mate. He begins to doubt their total understanding and begins to wonder about his faith in their love, and shatters their ideals.

The severing of communion causes a deep rift in their lives. They begin to misinterpret each other's actions, something that never occurred before, until it reaches the point where Justine feels she must leave to save his life. Once she is gone, however, he becomes increasingly aware of her absence and what she means to him. Yet, he refuses to act upon his longings and desires to bring her back. Although he desires to return to the life beyond, he cannot envision a way to mend the deeper spiritual union between them.

With Justine gone, he returns to thinking of Bessy (589). Although he realizes that if she was alive they could never be together, he continues to idealize her and her actions because she cannot return to destroy the fantasy. It is not until he learns Justine's actions had the root in his thoughts and ideals that he is willing to fight for her (606). Realizing that her leaving was her symbolic suicide for his love allows him to think that their souls were already united beyond (610). Once again, he needs a dead wife to realize the physical and spiritual union. This enables him to see his marriage to Justine as something above and beyond the physical and ordinary.

When he finally meets up with her, Justine looks ill and death-like. Her figure, instead of looking healthy, "suggested fatigue and languor...[H]er face was spent, extinguished—the very eyes were lifeless" (614). As he takes a closer look, he notices that her lips "had a slight bluish discoloration," and her mouth had "a tragic droop" (615). In other words, she is even starting to look dead. Her lips are turning blue like a corpse's, and her life force is extinguished from her face. Yet, seeing her in this death-like state provokes him to a physical expression of love. The more corpse-like she looks, the more he loves her. Only when her previous actions are recalled by the mention of a single word does he recoil from their closeness.

The life they return to, however, is just a shadow of the love they once had. If only Justine had literally died, like Lily Bart and Bessy, she would have been spared the final humiliation and been elevated to an idealized woman. Instead, she is forced to experience a public humiliation by watching the unveiling of Bessy's final selfish endeavor at the mills (627). Justine instantly recognizes the plans as Bessy's gym, created as an act of defiance against Amherst and to please the woman he hated. Finally, she realizes that "it was grotesque and pitiable that a man like Amherst should create out of his regrets a being who had never existed, and then ascribe to her feelings and actions which the real woman had again and again proved herself incapable!" (628). Justine finally realizes that the only way to win and keep his love is to be a dead and idealizable woman. The dead woman cannot shatter his idealized view of her through actions. In order to keep Amherst happy, she keeps the knowledge of Bessy's true intentions for the plans to herself. This secret, she realizes, is her final sacrifice for her "sins" to save Amherst's ideals (632).

As she is making this ultimate sacrifice, Amherst feels that he is reaching a new depth of feeling that he had never had before. He feels as if this is the moment he had been living for all his life, the defining moment of his life. Unfortunately for Justine, the moment is empty. She realizes that she will forever take a back seat to the dead woman in Amherst's life. The most she could hope for, if she wished to retain his love, is to become a dead, unchanging woman he could love for eternity. This ending is truly sad considering that "the novel is...filled with longing for a new relationship—one in which things of the mind are shared with a loved one" (Dwight 140). Not only were the characters feeling eternal longing, but when they did glimpse the union of ideals, it was quickly destroyed instead of cultivated. In spite of their quests, "neither woman finds the right formula for a more satisfying life" (Dyman 165). Amherst, however, does find the way to a happy life by ignoring the real woman and creating an ideal woman to love. The only thing this belief and behavior guarantees is a dead woman.

In depicting the relationships between Bessy and Amherst, and Justine and Amherst, Wharton is still working with the concepts of spiritual and physical love in a realm where society reinforces physical love even though the individual may desire a spiritual connection. Amherst destroys Bessy's love by his wanting a more complete union which includes a spiritual love. His partaking in a physical love with Bessy taints Justine's spiritual communion with him. Justine does come to a greater understanding of their situation, while Amherst elects to cling to his concept of the idealized woman. Although Justine is still alive at the end of the novel, one wonders if she might not be better off dead like Lily and Bessy. The next novel of Wharton's that we will discuss tackles that question. As we shall see, *Ethan Frome* presents the picture of what happens with the soul mate when her lover turns her into the living dead woman so that he can always have her by his side.

CHAPTER FIVE

Ethan Frome

Wharton began *Ethan Frome* as an exercise in French, but it soon "had grown into a long-legged hobbledehoy of a young novel" (Lewis & Lewis, 232). *Ethan Frome* is perhaps Wharton's darkest work, despite the fact that she "was *happy* while she was writing" it (Lewis 297). In spite of her personal happiness, Wharton's novella is one of completely destructive love, yet it also shows some changes in how she conceives of love. In this novella, Wharton's portrayal of love is at its darkest and deadliest. Ethan finds the love of similar souls and a physical love in one woman, but his desire to dominate her corrupts their potentially balanced love.

No longer is the male character just attracted to the dead or dying woman, but he also finds the woman who is alive and aflame with life attractive. Ethan finds in Mattie not only his soul mate who inspires him to a shared language, but also a physically desirable woman. Mattie's link to Ethan's soul reveals itself through her provoking him eloquence, making him feel "that words had at last been found to utter his secret soul . . ." (*Frome* 24). He describes his ideal soul mate in simple terms because he is a simple man. His soul mate is able to break the silence of his life and his soul. In fact, he believes she can evoke an eloquence from him, even though he rarely speaks. Unfortunately, Ethan's attraction not only evokes his spiritual passion, but also proves crippling to his lover as his love becomes a corrupting, almost vampiric, influence. In the process of draining the fire and life out of Mattie, he turns her into the living dead. In *Ethan Frome*, Wharton's conception of the interaction between love and death changes from the belief that the soul-mate can only be loved in death to the notion that a man can imagine both his physical love and his spiritual love in one person, yet both loves cannot exist simultaneously.

It is through the narrator's imagined story that Wharton's conception of the relation of love and death is dramatically enacted. At the story's opening, Ethan is married to Zeena, yet drawn to Mattie. His marriage, however, is far from ideal. Initially, her caretaking ability was a comfort in his loneliness. Yet, as she turns into a replacement for his mother, her presence becomes a hindrance to him achieving a fuller love with Mattie. Keeping in line with the concept of death being connected to love, death surrounds his proposal and subsequent marriage to Zeena since these actions were prompted by of the death of his mother in the dead of winter (51). There is no romance in this marriage for Ethan. He is not in love with her, he does not find her beautiful and, most interestingly, he proposes because of death. He marries her because he felt obligated to her (51). Zeena agrees that she was entitled to marry him others told her she was entitled to the marriage proposal after all she had done to assist him (80). In spite of her feeling that it was expected for him to marry her, he really was not aware of the implications of having her as a wife (51). All he truly knew is that if she had left, he would be alone. So, in the dead of winter, in the aftermath of his mother's death, Ethan weds Zeena. He marries because the one woman in his life was now dead and another physical presence, another care-taker, must save him from loneliness.

Zeena does not have the physical ornamentation that would make her a desirable mate according to sexual selection. Her key attributes are, however, her ability to replace Ethan's dead mother and become his care-taker for life. It could be argued, that his attraction to her voice and speech could be a form of appreciation for the "song" used to attract mates according to sexual selection. Darwin argues that "females...use their voices as a love call" to attract males (2:332). Through music and song a female "awakens the gentler feelings of tenderness and love, which readily pass into devotion" (2:335). In fact, "the suspicion does not appear improbably that the progenitors of man, either the males or females, or both sexes, before they had acquired the power of expressing their mutual love in articulate language, endeavoured to charm each other with musical notes and rhythm" (2:337). Although it can be argued that Zeena's speech acted like a song to entice him, the devotion that Darwin predicts should follow, does not (51). Ethan does believe her voice provides a relief from "the mortal silence of his long imprisonment," but he still does not love her (51). Interestingly, we rarely hear her speaking prior to their marriage. If Zeena's speech was seductive music to his ears, there is no real proof. Shortly after their marriage, she falls silent. On the rare occasions that she does speak, he elects to ignore or dismiss her. It confuses Frome when she no longer talks, just like what happened with his mother. Essentially, he becomes confused when she becomes the woman he created. He devised a history for her that she completely accepted and adopted instead of fighting him to create her own story. In submitting to her fate, Zeena becomes the woman Ethan's mother was prior to her death. At this point, she closes herself off to him and any hope of sexual passion disappears.

Ethan cannot comprehend his role in creating these silent, deadly women. Instead, he believes that farm life is what drove them to silence, not his neglect (52). After all, isolation and hard physical labor is their life in Starkfield. Zeena also gives him another reason for her falling silent. She reveals to him that she stopped talking because he stopped listening (53). Unfortunately, Zeena is not connected to Ethan's soul to allow for them to have an unspoken communication. Her silence is from neglect, not a greater bond. Because there is no essential bond between them, he reads her silence as a sign of her becoming like his mother. Ethan justifies his neglect of her appeals for a physical love by placing the blame on her, not himself. Eventually, his neglect of her manifests itself in physical elements on their farm. The land begins to falter and the center section of the house must be removed (13). With the removal of the heart of the house, they have lost their "warmth and nourishment" (13). Even the cucumber-vine on the porch is "dead [and] dangled…like a crape streamer tied to the door for death" (37). Although later he would like to imagine the vine commemorating Zeena's death, it is their physical love which is dead.

Soon all Ethan believes of Zeena is that she is a body who cares for bodies. Her medical knowledge, gathered through caring for her own body, draws even greater attention to her physical concerns. In fact, all of her illnesses, most of which occur whenever Ethan indulges in his attraction to Mattie, focus one's attention to her body. Zeena, for the majority of the novella, is a physical entity without a voice or spirit. Although at one time she was subject to impulses, much like Bessy Westmore in *The Fruit of the Tree*, her illnesses have forced her into relative inactivity. Her rare impulses combined with her even rarer vocalizations cause Ethan pain. These actions are her way of asserting her life and desires which Ethan denies to see her as a replacement for his mother, instead of a potential lover. So, in order to ease his pain, he turns Zeena into a body at the expense of the rest of her. In fact, she begins to use her body to communicate with him. When she needs his attention or is troubled by something concerning him, her body asserts itself, keeping her awake and in enough pain to visit the doctor's office.

Eventually, when Zeena inserts herself too much into Ethan's desired life, he hopes that vandals will come and destroy her body. He begins to hate her body. Her presence becomes another responsibility left to him after his father's demise (50). Her body becomes a physical manifestation of illness and death as the light reveals "her puckered throat and projecting wrist...and [the light] deepened fantastically the hollows and prominences of her high-boned face" (38). In a way, this is the final step in her becoming the replacement for his dead mother; she becomes a walking embodiment of his mother's corpse. She takes on the role he created for her and it has ruined her, turning her into the bitter crone his mother once was. Ethan, much like when his mother took ill, is unprepared to deal with another ill woman. The revelation that Zeena has changed comes as a shock to him, so much so, that he felt he had never really seen her before (38).

Interestingly, Zeena's body carries the blame for Ethan's failed dreams, much as his mother's carries the blame for his marrying Zeena. Her body becomes the reason for him not living up to his potential and having to relinquish his dreams of a greater life for a life on the farm. Unfortunately, the facts are not in complete agreement with Ethan's story. Initially, Zeena was willing, and in her way demanding, that they leave the farming life Ethan had known. She never desired to be a farm wife, but wanted a different world for herself and her husband (52). Yet, he fails in selling the farm. Instead of admitting his failure, he blames Zeena for their predicament. He convinces himself that they could not move because she would not be admired by others in a larger city (52). Zeena, however, had already given up her identity in marrying Ethan and becoming his replacement mother figure. She originally was from a city bigger than Starkfield and perhaps wanted to see an even bigger environment. It is Ethan, in actuality, who would lose his identity in a big city. People in the big city would no longer see him as the wonderful, caring son struggling to make the family farm profitable, as Starkfield views him. He turns Zeena, more specifically her body, into the culprit because he does not want to admit his own fears and failures. She becomes tainted, just as his marrying as a result of his mother's death taints his mother's image. In his version of their story, she figuratively emasculates him; she drains him of his goals and dreams.

Once Mattie enters his life, Ethan's world changes. Whatever satisfaction and comfort Zeena may have once provided is no longer sufficient to maintain his happiness because he has found a woman of fire and light, capable of receiving his love. Her presence brings both of the Fromes back to life at different points in the novella (Wershoven 21). Her initial appearance categorizes her as being full of light and fire (23). She is, in effect, alive. Her light, her youth, and the fact that "he could show her things and tell her things, and taste the bliss of feeling that all he imparted left long reverberations and echoes he could wake at will" was very attractive to Ethan (23). He delights that their communication goes beyond the physical level to the spiritual connection he had missed with Zeena. In essence, Ethan feels that Mattie finds the words "to utter his secret soul" (24). His soul has been the one thing that Zeena was never able to reach. Instead of trying, she became a silent replacement for his mother. Interestingly, although Mattie is attractive and can reach his soul, she cannot have both his physical and spiritual love without becoming a crippled, death-like crone.

As if to emphasize these two loves being centered within Mattie, when he first sees her at the dance, she is wearing a "cherry-coloured" scarf (21). While he is in this voyeuristic role, her physical desirability takes precedence over her spiritual desirability. Not only does the fascinator draw attention to Mattie's entire head as an erogenous zone, it also serves to show that her mind, as well as her body, fascinates him. Because he is not talking to her, she cannot reach his soul and his physical love begins to dominate his image of her. He even begins to see other men as competition for her attention. Ethan does have the power to attract, just not with his beauty. Even the narrator finds Ethan to be the most intriguing and promising figure in town (1). The fact that the narrator finds Ethan so appealing is somewhat surprising. Frome is not handsome by any means; his face is harsh and his body looks old beyond his years (1). Yet, in spite of Frome's ghostly physical appearance, the narrator is more interested in him than in any other person. His physical deformities also cause the narrator to create a love story for Frome to account for his "careless powerful look" (1). It is interesting, and perhaps very reflective of the narrator's mind, that he feels that Frome's strength and deformity stem from destructive romantic relationships, not the futile long hours he spent on the farm, even though farm life is a more likely cause.

As soon as Ethan sees another man's passionate desire for Mattie, the scarf falls from her head, symbolic of a deflowering. The fact that another man is interested in Mattie's body, not her mind, is repugnant to Ethan. Dennis Eady's physical passion forces Ethan to confront his own budding physical love for her. Eady's desire for her body over her spirit, however, makes Mattie appear cheapened. For Ethan, Mattie regains her privileged status by rejecting Dennis to walk home with Ethan. In his eyes, she has selected him as her ideal mate. His constant preoccupation with her hair emphasizes Ethan's love for her. Even after the near-fatal sleigh ride, Ethan is not aware of Mattie's mangled body, but he is aware of the wounded sounds she makes and of her hair. In being able to find both loves in Mattie, Ethan continues along the path Wharton began with Amherst. However, where Amherst eventually destroys the love of Justine's soul for him, Ethan will destroy Mattie's body. Perhaps this is because "Mattie lacks the wit and critical intelligence of many other" characters, so does Ethan (Wershoven 22). It could be that her intellectual lack causes a corresponding lack in the vocabulary necessary to create a Republic. Without the expressed Republic, the only thing left to destroy is the physical.

When they are together, Mattie's presence evokes a desire for a truly common language from Ethan (35). Zeena never had this effect on him. Even prior to their marriage, Zeena could not touch his soul to evoke any kind of verbal expression from him. After their marriage, she only evokes a deadly silence in him. Although Mattie does inspire him to expressiveness, he cannot actually act upon her inspiration. The most expressive speech he is capable of is "a growl of rapture" as he says the words "Come along" (32). Ethan's early attempts to express himself are in the form of this Darwinian, animalistic growl because speech is so rare for him. Although he desires to be a man who can express his innermost feelings with a worthy soul mate, the primitive growl is his only means of expression at this point. Mattie's role in his expressiveness makes him believe that "all his life was lived in the sight and sound of Mattie Silver" (28). There is no life left for him outside of Mattie's influence. However, his marriage to Zeena demands that it must be otherwise. There is no conceivable way for him to be with both Mattie and Zeena.

Death envelops Ethan as he is learning to balance the physical love and the love for her soul. Mattie reveals that the happy lovers, Ned and Ruth, were almost killed earlier that day, the farm houses look like headstones in a cemetery to him on their walk (32), and he hugs Mattie surrounded by his dead ancestors burial ground (36). It is typical for Wharton to have the first buds of romance bloom when surrounded by death. Ethan even annexes the dead as accomplices in keeping Mattie in his life. As he tells her they will never be apart, he enlists the help of "the dead, lovers once . . ." to help him keep his promise (36). One has to wonder if Ethan feels that these dead lovers are the ideal and if he would be successful in his courtship without the aura of death around him. Ethan, it seems, cannot find love except when surrounded by the aura of death. Ethan's love for Mattie can only be vocalized in the wake of death, much like Selden expressed love for Lily when she was dead.

Although he did have the chance to pursue Mattie away from the deadly aura, he failed to seize the opportunity. During the spring picnic, he did not have the courage to approach her in the manner he desired. Their encounter at the church picnic provided Ethan an opportunity with Mattie while surrounded by youthful happiness in the summer. As with many of Wharton's lovers and their Republic of the Spirit up to this point in her works, the images of summers and streams encompass moments of their highest communion. In an interesting twist, Ethan can only experience the significance of the summer scene in the winter while surrounded by the dead, essentially reliving a moment that is dead and gone from them. Instead of speaking his feelings previously, even though she was receptive, he shrank from his opportunity until they revisit the spot in the dead of winter. Only then does he feel that he and Mattie sat in "inarticulate…happiness" remembering their summer encounter (111). He even works up the nerve to tell her she was pretty that summer and he "had the illusion that he was a free man, wooing the girl he meant to marry" (112). When she desires to leave, Ethan realizes that he cannot tell her all he wishes "in that place of summer memories" (112). He can neither envision nor express a love with his soul mate unless it is entered into in an aura of death. It is only in the atmosphere of the dead and the support of the dead lovers that he can indulge in dreams of the first time he put his arm around her as "they walked on as if they were floating on a summer stream" (37). After this closeness with Mattie, Ethan refuses to taint it with Zeena's presence. Instead, he tries to maintain the illusion of Mattie's nearness and lightness.

Once Zeena is absent, the house becomes a home to Ethan and Mattie. In fact, their entire world seems to change as if a spell was cast over them. Their home is not the dark, dreary, arid farm without its center, but a place of light and life. Both Ethan and Mattie are heard singing. The sun is streaming in through the kitchen window, providing warmth and light. Their home life becomes an idealized version of life. Mattie becomes a romanticized wife and creates a whole new universe for Ethan. He is shocked at what a change Zeena's absence brings (49). With Zeena gone, the mother figure has also left and he can begin to live an adult life. Upon returning after work, Ethan confronts the fact that the change may not be as radical as he was hoping as he finds the door locked as it was the previous night. He is relieved to discover that the youthful body which greets him belongs to Mattie (59). Mattie appearing with a red ribbon in her hair, reminiscent of the scarf, allows Ethan to feel "suffocated with the sense of well being" (59). Thus, he even sees this delightful experience of light and warmth as tinged with death. Her presence, however, almost kills him with positive feelings and the hope of a new life. His linking of his happiness with suffocation is expected, given that moments of his highest physical desire for Mattie are surrounded by death and destruction. She reawakens his physical love with the sexually symbolic meal she prepares. The fire in the hearth is reminiscent of the dance hall as his heart beat faster and he desired to see her in the light. Just as he imagined a glowing flash passing between the dancers earlier, he believes there is a spark between them. He fails to act on his desires at dinner, just as he was unable to act on them at the dance.

Unfortunately, their time alone in the house is just a shadow of the Republic. As they grow closer, some form of Zeena interrupts their communion by making Ethan paralyzed with fear and inaction. They feel her interruption destroys their budding bond just as they watch the cat break her pickle dish earlier. Ethan's entering a position of control over the situation causes him to feel as if "his soul swelled with pride as he saw how his tone subdued her. . . Except when he was steering a big log down the mountain to his mill he had never known such a thrilling sense of mastery" (63). In being able to control her tears, Ethan feels a sexual power over her as the phallic imagery suggests. By linking the wild log ride to his mastery over Mattie, Ethan shows that he wants to domesticate her in order to keep her. He also believes that his sexual dominance over her will aid in the domestication he feels she needs. He had often thought that marriage would bring out her wifely instincts, but since he will not relinquish his hold on her to another man, Ethan feels he must domesticate the wild in her. However, he acknowledges that Mattie has no interest in hypothetical wifely duties (25).

After Ethan's being able to feel a sexual power over her, their conversation gives him the peacefulness and "illusion of long-established intimacy which no outburst of emotion could have given . . ." (65). Instead, they bond while discussing mundane, daily issues. While watching her, impressions of both her mind and body enter his mind. He is fascinated with the impact his words have upon her physical features. He even thinks she looks "like a wheat-field under a summer breeze. It was intoxicating to find such magic in his clumsy words" (66). Ethan's comparing her face to a wheat field takes on an ominous tone when one considers that as a farmer, he has not done well by his land. Although he is able to eke out a living from his fields, they are, for the most part, dead. Yet, there is also hope of fruitfulness, albeit a slim hope, as long as someone cares for and nurtures the land. By equating Mattie to the land, Wharton provides a clue to Mattie's gruesome ending. Ethan will reap her body and spirit, just as he reaps the fields at harvest. The hope of fruitfulness for Mattie will be gone.

No matter how much Mattie is able to intoxicate him with her "enchanted" speech, she cannot save herself from Ethan's deadly desire (67). He turns the magic of words into a deadly venture as he changes the conversation to sledding and the near-death of Ruth and Ned and foreshadows their sled ride towards the end of the novella. What should have been a happy, exhilarating moment for the lovers becomes almost fatal. By putting Mattie in danger, either verbally through their conversation of near death, or physically, by leaving clues so Zeena will dismiss her, Ethan gains his power. Yet, as he gains his power over her, the "ancient implications of conformity and order" are evoked, making him feel like she is drifting away from him (67). Thus, by invoking the traditional male-female, husband-wife power roles, Ethan moves his soul-mate farther from his reach, by not allowing her to be his equal. Instead, she is someone he wishes to dominate.

Ethan, however, like many of Wharton's male characters, is content to live with the fantasy of life with Mattie (71). He is happy that he did not act on his physical love so that their spiritual love can still be pure, uncorrupted by lesser lustful feelings. It was his desire to keep his image of her pure. He did, however, taint the image for her with his desire to domesticate her and have sexual power over her. He is content with the vision only as long as it allows him to deny reality, to deny the fact that Zeena is his wife and Mattie is nothing, in the traditional sense, to him. In the light of day, when he can no longer deny reality, he finds himself incapable of telling her his desires (72).

Zeena's return from the doctor's office imposes her body upon the world created by Ethan and Mattie, both physically by her presence and verbally, in her discussing her body's diseases. Her expressing that her illness is worse than Ethan suspects is her way of asserting her claims over her husband and brings her closer to what his mother was like when she was called in to help (77). Interestingly, once she says this, he no longer fantasizes about her death. Instead, he feels compassion and fear that her words may actually be true. The compassion does not last long as Zeena exercises her ability to separate Ethan and Mattie completely and forever. Ethan thinks her causing this separation transforms her from "the listless creature who had lived at his side in a state of sullen self-absorption" to "a mysterious alien presence, an evil energy" that has been hidden for years (84–85). Zeena drains the power from Ethan and demonstrates that her physicality puts her in control, and he hates her for that. Her actions revive his believe that she is keeping him from his full potential in all parts of life. His inability to save his soul mate by changing the situation shows that his power was a figment of his imagination. In his mind, Zeena is killing all his hopes and desires. He envisions that she will never let him be happy.

The fear of losing Mattie pushes him to physical actions he had never thought of acting on before. He finally kisses her, "drinking unconsciousness of everything but the joy [her lips] gave him. She lingered for a moment, caught in the same strong current; then slipped from him…pale and troubled" (86). This kiss becomes a vampire's bite as he drains her of her color, turning her into a pale, death-like woman. Their first kiss transforms her from the ethereal light of the sun to the pale and troubled physical woman. As this transformation takes place, "he saw her drowning in a dream" (86). In order to try to save her he cries out to her, finally able to state what he was feeling about her from the beginning. While retaining this image he has the feeling of their kiss, yet it is a feeling that leaves him wanting more (87). The more he focuses upon the kiss, the more deadly physical Mattie becomes. His thoughts and actions vampirically feast upon her fire and sunlight.

Both of Ethan's ways of living, the dreary existence with Zeena and the light-filled existence with Mattie, come to a climax when Zeena discovers the broken pickle dish. She accuses Mattie of trying to take everything from her (91). Overtly, these comments refer to the broken dish, but Zeena could just as well be talking about Mattie trying to take Ethan from her by reawakening in him the hopes and dreams that he believed Zeena stole from him. Zeena's pain and tears, however, do not evoke compassion from Ethan. At a time when he should be feeling compassion for her, he feels nothing because Mattie has become his ideal love.

Although Ethan desires to escape with Mattie, his concerns for both Mattie's and Zeena's welfare stop him. He begins to believe there is no way out of his current situation (97). He forever sees himself bound to Zeena's body making him unable to envision a world where he and Mattie can be together. The next morning, while Mattie and Ethan agonized over at the thought of their impending separation, Zeena is more animate and lively (99). While they are suffering the pain of separation, Zeena becomes alive, almost as if she is actually thriving on their misery. As they deteriorate, both physically and emotionally, she regains her physical health. This return to health prepares her for their ending, where she will become the mother figure and caretaker to them both.

As she grows stronger, Ethan begins to lose the eloquence Mattie had awakened in him. This loss spurs him, finally, to be able to speak to Zeena. He speaks not words of love and devotion, but of defiance. In essence, he tries to assert his power over Zeena. This change in Ethan makes Zeena's deathly physicality reassert itself as her illness returns (109). When Ethan and Mattie are finally able to communicate again, it is to communicate a death wish. Ethan expresses his desire to "a'most rather have you [Mattie] dead than" to lose her (114). Her accepting his wishes for her leads to their final near-fatal act of defiance; the only overt expression of their love.

Their freedom in death allows them to never be separated, recalling the romantic dead lovers of the past. They would be expressing the totality of their love once and forever to the entire world. Ethan agrees to the romantic death wish because he sees it as their way to be together along with being the ultimate act of his power over her. This desire to be together forever, to share every element of their lives, could, for them, only be attained in death. Their final kiss seems to take them to "the pond together in the burning August sun" while surrounded by the cold and deadly winter (120). As the coldness of their situation engulfs them, the "blackness and silence" make them feel like "they might have been in their coffins underground" (120). Their passionate embrace is the embrace of death. At the height of their romance, they not only feel the heat and living of summer, but are also surrounded by the cold and death of the Starkfield winter.

The grave coast down the hill brings them the closest to a communion they will ever feel and brings them closest to the Republic of the Spirit. Wharton describes them as flying high above their world, much like the descriptions of entering the Republic of the Spirit found in earlier works. Ethan feels "that they were flying indeed, flying far up into the cloudy night, with Starkfield immeasurably below them . . ." (122). Yet, the image of the two of them sledding also recalls the earlier one of Ethan riding the logs (63). Instead of them reaching a union of one soul loving another, the physical desire interrupts, and perhaps corrupts their ideal spiritual union by bringing it back to physical love. Eventually, he feels that "her blood seemed to be in his veins" (122). At this point, he feels they are one body. Their common language and spiritual bond are second to the primacy of the physical. Zeena, however, interrupts their physical union, just as she did earlier at their dinner party.

In the end, the tree does not provide for the death they wished. Instead of freeing their souls to unite together, it traps them in their now ruined bodies. After the accident, Mattie is no longer the sun and fire, but "her hair was as grey as her companion's, her face as bloodless and shriveled...her body kept its limp immobility, and her dark eyes had the bright witch-like stare..." (125). Their attempt to fulfill the romantic death wish turns Mattie into the feared crone and Ethan is physically, and perhaps emotionally, crippled. Ethan's "right" side is "shortened and warped" (2). Much as his dreams were cut short by his intellectual failing, so his body and "right" way of life and love were cut short by the sledding accident.

Zeena, however, rises above her physical illnesses to care for them both. Even Mrs. Hale recounts that Zeena, despite her illness, "had the strength given her to care for those two for over twenty years, and before the accident came she thought she even couldn't care for herself" (129). It appears as if her good health comes at the expense of Mattie's and Ethan's. She becomes the vampire, feeding off of the misery of the lovers. Ethan and Mattie, in seeking death in love and love in death, kill their romance. However, it is not until the narrator arrives that there is someone able to tell the story of their ill-fated love. Mrs. Hale sees the ultimate pity in the love story of Ethan and Mattie. She realizes that if Mattie "ha' died, Ethan might ha' lived; and the way they are now, I don't see's there's much difference between the Fromes up at the farm and the Fromes down in the graveyard" (130). Mrs. Hale and the narrator see that death, or at least a death-like existence, is all that is left for the Frome household. Mattie's fate brings to mind Justine's actions for Bessy in *The Fruit of the Tree*. Whereas Bessy had someone willing to put an end to her suffering, thus allowing Amherst to idealize his love for her, Mattie is not that lucky. Instead, she must live a life where people feel sorry for her.

In his attempts to find a balanced love with Mattie, Ethan not only damages her body, but her soul, turning her into the owner of a voice that is a "querulous drone" (125). She is not the source of inspiration any more. She cannot evoke expressive speech from him. In attempting to dominate Mattie, as he has with the other women in his life, he destroys her for any other man. Zeena, Mattie and Ethan live in misery because they can never strike a balanced love. When Zeena was healthy, Mattie was suffering, growing pale and dying. The reverse was also true. As Mattie becomes fire and sunlight for Ethan, Zeena grows physically ill. Given the narrator's description of Mattie and Zeena at the end of the novel, the women appear to be isolated parts that do not make a whole. For the narrator, Mattie ends up a soul trapped in a hideously disfigured body. She can speak and think, but cannot move on her own. Zeena suffers a similar, but perhaps worse, fate. She becomes a body whose lover has neglected her soul for so long that it has fled her. She ignores Mattie's complaints, and has no life or spark of soul in her eyes (125). Although in the end they all exist in the same room, there is no way for them all to live together healthily and happily. This unhealthy, unholy trinity is what Ethan's love creates. Although he can have both the physical love and the spiritual love in his life with Mattie's presence, she suffers the fate of a near dead crone. Her figurative death enables Ethan to keep her and his mother figure in his life together.

Instead of being blind to spiritual love, Ethan's eyes are open to both physical and spiritual elements of love. Yet, when he tries to have power over his loves, he destroys them. Although he believes he is seeking a balanced love, he fails to achieve it, just as he has failed to achieve the greatness he felt destined for in the big city. The tension we see here will be enacted to a fuller extent in the novels which follow. Neither Zeena, nor

Mattie, nor Ethan has found an everlasting happiness. This sad, crippled ending shows that Wharton still had not come to terms with both spiritual love and physical love. The two cannot exist in life to bring about a complete and total happiness. In fact, those who seek both end up crippled and crippling their love. Wharton begins to question the desire for a balanced love as a destructive force in the next novel, *The Reef*. Although Ethan's leaning more towards a love of souls and the ability to dominate Mattie physically, Anna Leath will confront the potential emptiness of a love of souls at the expense of the physical.

CHAPTER SIX

The Reef

Wharton turned from the dark, dreary world of *Ethan Frome* to the primacy of physical love in her next work, *The Reef*. In this novel, we not only see the conflict between the physical and spiritual love as found in *Ethan Frome*, but we also see the foreshadowing of the heightened physical passion which will emerge in *Summer*. With the ascendance of the importance of physical love, the image of the death-like or dead lover fades into the background. In fact, those who desire the physical love are the ones who are the healthiest and happiest. Anna Leath is the first of Wharton's female characters who wants to change by experiencing "the stuff of human experience" she felt she did not have in her earlier life without sacrificing a belief in spiritual love (Wharton, *The Reef* 269). Yet, the physical passion is more troubling in *The Reef* than in the later work. Wharton does not come to a stable, solid conclusion regarding spiritual and physical love in this work. Instead, she depicts the conflict that occurs when one desires both without a balance. There is also a change from her earlier works where lovers can find love, a true fulfilling union, only in death. Whereas Sophy finds happiness and fulfillment in a physical love, Anna can only find a qualified happiness in being torn between physical and spiritual love. Anna's dilemma reflects Wharton's questions regarding wanting a physical love over a love of souls, which is unresolved at the end of the novel.

For many readers, Wharton's concerns regarding her relationships are examined throughout the novel (Benstock, Erlich, Lewis). Also, it has not gone unnoticed that passion is at the center of the work (Erlich, Miller Hadley, Levine, Wolff). Bert Bender, however, sees the main crux of the novel as a conflict between a "highly civilized woman committed to preserving her idealized love" coming face-to-face "with the dark truth" of Darwinian sexual selection and sexuality (329). It is, in fact, the conflict between a spiritual love being in direct opposition to a physical (Darwinian) love with which Anna must struggle. In spite of the fact that Darrow and Anna have always felt they belonged to each other, whenever they are on the verge of entering into a permanent relationship, she constantly places obstacles in their way. Although early on in their lives she felt Darrow would help her "find the magic bridge" (92) needed in her life, she felt that his lust for Kitty Mayne distanced them so that he would never understand her. Anna believes that Darrow's lust for another woman, a purely physical woman, corrupts him. Kitty, according to Anna, does not have the mind and spirit to attract a man, but she does have the excessive physicality that men seem to desire. This knowledge sent Anna to the arms of Fraiser Leath, who she thought had the imagination capable of meeting her soul in love, and delayed her relationship with Darrow for twelve years. Having an imagination to see the finer things in life should recall Lily's chief complaint about Percy Gryce in *The House of Mirth*. Although Lily was able to see that Gryce lacked imagination, Anna was unable to see this lack in Fraiser until after their marriage.

When the novel opens, the most recent obstacle in their union is Anna delaying Darrow's arrival at her home, Givré, for the second time. After she relegates him to a passive role in his relationship with her, Sophy provides Darrow with an outlet for active interaction so that he finally gets to be in control of his romantic relationship, even if it is only a purely physical one. Her distress at the train station allows him to save her. When explaining to Anna the reasons for his actions, he draws upon this desire to be active, to be meaningful to a woman (268). Anna has denied him this fundamental desire. In doing so, she denies him an outlet to show his strength and traits which make him a good mate according to sexual selection. Sophy, it turns out, gave him someone to rescue and assist in a way that Anna would not allow him (268). Sophy, in essence, permits him to be the strong man he thinks he is, while Anna forces him to be an idealized version of a man.

What he never expected, however, was that his tryst with Sophy would so completely and totally impact his ideal spiritual love with Anna. He does not realize that his past physical loves had the same effect in slowly chipping away at his chances of his ideal love. Kitty Mayne and Lady Ulrica Crispin show his predisposition for finding entertaining diversions with women of life and passion, but they are not what he truly desires. They, along with Sophy, are among the girls Anna felt were living the same life as she was, but having different experiences and knowing different secrets (91). For Anna, the world is comprised of those who had the soul to see the beauty of the soul and those who knew the secret of physical love. In being able to see the beauty of things, Anna is in the realm of Plato's soul love (*Phaedrus* 36, *Symposium* 54). This beauty in her world is a beauty of the soul over the body, yet now she wants to learn more. These two approaches to life represent distinct and divergent views, but they are also her two versions of love. Anna must still discover the physical love found in sexual selection; the physical passion that the rest of the world knows. What she wishes from Darrow is that he will teach her this lesson.

He is an aficionado of physical love, as shown by his previous adventures and his desire to link Sophy to this life at their first meeting. Although she has the beauty to make her desirable in terms of sexual selection, the fact that he feels his sexual desire for her aroused makes her less than the idealized soul mate he desires in Anna (27). Despite her beauty and lightness, he knows Sophy will never be his spiritual soul mate. She lacks the imagination that he and Anna share. Darrow's inability to remember she was a member of the house of assignation he visited with Lady Ulrica, reveals his desire to repress his sexual desire, though the physical draws him. Sophy, although a beauty, is not memorable because she is a fixture in the house of physical pleasures. Once he does realize where he had seen her, he is only able to place her as "one of the shadowy sliding presences in the background" of his pursuit of Lady Ulrica (28). In relegating her to the shadows, he demonstrates that she is not worthy of his full attention. In order for him to have any sort of relationship with Sophy, he must distance her from the world of excessive physicality, but not completely. Yet, she still must be enough of a lady for his desire for her not to be offensive to him, but not a complete lady since he does not want her as his soul mate. Although Sophy does move to the forefront during their short time together in the city, once they have parted, she slides back into the darkness.

However, while they are together, she awakens his appreciation for a free life where they can acknowledge and embrace their physicality. Her companionship makes him free from restraints (28). Sophy has elected to live a life on the margins by indulging her physical nature. The ideals of the imagination do not bind her as she actually strives to live life to its fullest. In fact, Darrow had never met anyone quite like her in all his adventures. His previous trysts with Kitty Mayne and Lady Crispin were with women who were also touched by the upbringing that Anna experienced. Yet, despite Darrow's awakening to a new way of life, Sophy's way of life, she will always remain an entertainment for him, nothing more (30). She is not on the same level as Darrow and cannot be able to participate in a greater union with him because she is free in a way he cannot comprehend. She is not his soul mate, but she is a pleasant diversion.

In dramatic contrast to Anna's views of physicality, Darrow's trysts with other women do not offend Sophy. In fact, she and Jimmy Brance had frequently discussed the extent of Darrow's passion for the woman as if it were a matter-of-fact occurrence. Sophy even used the conversation to entice Jimmy by telling him she speculated about what Lady Ulrica and Darrow had done (31). Sophy is not only in touch with her physical desires, but she also knows how others react to physical situations. She does not shy away from the physical love between two people, but embraces it and uses it to her advantage with Jimmy. Unlike Anna, Sophy knows that physical love should be embraced and acknowledged, not denied.

For Sophy, actions, not denials and renunciations, are the way to experience love and life. She does not fall victim to the romantic notion of a spiritual love being able to unite loved ones; instead, she would rather have demonstrative actions as a show of love and admiration. Once Darrow learns of Sophy's views, he sees her face as oscillating between "a field of daisies in a summer breeze" and "the hard stamp of experience" (35). He does not really know how to experience Sophy's life because she is unlike any woman he has met before. She has all the elements of being a lady, but the experience which chills her in her prime. Sophy's experience stems from her ability to act upon her physical love instead of pretending it is dead. It is because she realizes the necessity of living physicality that she is able to see her much-married sister as embodying romance (35). What Anna comes to believe is offensive, Sophy sees as opportunities for a great new life and love.

Darrow's acquaintance with Sophy begins at a time in his life when he feels he "no longer understood the violent impulses and dreamy pauses of his own young heart" (38). Just because he does not care to understand the actions of his heart does not mean that they no longer possess him. What it does mean, however, is that he feels his recent experiences with Anna have deadened him to desire the knowledge of his heart. Her inability to allow him into her life has had a deadening effect upon his feelings and emotions, his heart and passion. Yet, Sophy has the power to awaken him to the elements Anna deadens. His time with Sophy shows him the reality of a physical life can be as rewarding as living in an idealized world. He does acknowledge that she is radically different from the women he has known in the past, from women like Anna (38). It is her freedom which enables her to live an active life and remind him of the actual physicality he had once enjoyed with other women.

Once he convinces himself of Sophy's being free, he feels she reawakens his passionate side. He lives for experiences, to give her experiences, she had never had before. He is not interested in her mind, but in her physical responses. He delights in being awake to serving her, a feeling that Anna tried to stifle in him (44). To Darrow, this is just a temporary escape from the passive world in which Anna had forced him. He does not plan to spend his entire life with Sophy. In fact, he sees her just as a diversion since he had already made the trip. He is, however, grateful for this diversion (44). However, she does not even tempt him to a greater, longer-lasting, spiritual relationship. She is just an adventure, similar to the adventures and experiments that Lawrence Selden had in *The House of Mirth*. Whether Sophy thought the adventure would end in sexual fulfillment or something more permanent, such as marriage, Darrow keeps his view of the situation as a brief adventure, not meant for anything more. The adventure, in his mind, will not affect his intended life with Anna. Instead, Sophy exists just as a passing diversion and make him feel better about himself.

In order to support more fully his notion of their relationship, Darrow believes that Sophy misses out on the "beauty of things" (45). This is the opposite of Anna, who sees the beauty in things, but has missed out on the essence of life. While driving back to the hotel, he thinks, "she did not feel the beauty and mystery of the spectacle as much as its pressure of human significance, all its hidden implication of emotion and adventure" (45). She will never have the finer taste to awaken her to the beauty around her, but she is aware of the other side of life. Later at the theater, he feels the same belief about her as he thinks that she is more concerned with the plot than the deeper meaning of life (69). In essence, he thinks she is focused on living life, not thinking about what lies beyond. Not only does Sophy not have the imagination, the mind, the spirit to grasp the greater beauty of the play, but there is also no hope of her ever awakening to the Republic of the Spirit that

Wharton's previous characters had thought was the ultimate place for their love. Sophy is all human physicality, not ethereal soul. Yet, she does feel physical love with an intensity that others would miss.

Although he feels that they were growing closer and it was easy to explain things to her (47), the thought of a world away from Anna makes him want to flee. His desire is still for a woman like Anna who can see beauty where others see none because that type of woman offers him a love beyond the physical. The adventure with Sophy is just that, a fleeting adventure. Her presence and needs serve to raise his self-esteem. He is able to define himself, for a short time at least, in relation to how he served her. However, as long as he has hopes of success with Anna, Sophy will be a lesser vision to him. When there are no letters from Anna, Sophy occupies a larger place in his heart and eyes (56). It is not that she has suddenly changed, but the fact that he needs a woman to help him define his self-worth that makes her more interesting. Yet, defining himself in terms of Sophy causes Darrow to change. Soon he begins to know "the primitive complacency of the man" with a companion for which other men feel lust (58). Her use to him is in that she is a symbol of physical love. All men want her because she is desirable. This is a feeling he will never experience with Anna. Her place is not to be physically desirable, but to be spiritually desirable only to one man, her soul mate, Darrow. In the end, he fails to post Sophy's letter because he cannot bear to be without a woman to reflect his self-worth.

During their initial time together, Darrow felt that their relationship alternated between camaraderie and a physical love (61). His feelings for Sophy also change as his feelings for Anna change. When things appear to be promising with Anna, Darrow convinces himself that his feelings toward Sophy are those of friendship. When there is trouble in his relationship with Anna, Sophy becomes his physical love. Once Anna's silence has completely disillusioned him; Darrow's

> imagination continued to follow her [Sophy] to and fro, traced the curve of her slim young arms as she raised them to undo her hair, pictured the sliding down of her dress to the waist and then to the knees, and the whiteness of her feet as she slipped across the floor to bed...(64–65)

This scene becomes the first truly erotic image he allows himself to have of Sophy. She no longer is just the girl he keeps around to brighten up his dull loneliness while waiting for his soul mate to call. Instead, she becomes a physical experiment for him, a way for him to step into the life Anna's love forces him to deny in order to have their spiritual love. This erotic image is new in Wharton's works. In previous works such as *Ethan Frome*, she relied on symbolic images of sexual desire. Ethan's log ride and Mattie's symbolic dinner is mild compared to Darrow's allowing his mind to caress Sophy's naked body. Interestingly this change toward the erotic images brings about a corresponding in the use of imagination. Darrow's imagination does not draw him to lofty heights with Sophy, but to a physical union.

It is at the theater, where "the ghosts of actors" seen through Sophy's eyes transform acting to reality that he feels the full extent of Sophy's effect upon him (67). She re-awakens him to life and physical love which he had set aside in his pursuit of his soul mate. He channels his imagination to the one type of love which he thinks is available to him. When he discovers that Sophy is as unhappy as he is, Darrow believes that they should act on their physical love. They become united though unhappiness, not shared thoughts or souls. In an ironic twist, it is only after he finally acknowledges his physical love for Sophy that Anna breaks her silence. He then feels the pressure of the selection between physical love with Sophy and spiritual love with Anna. As if to emphasize the choices before Darrow, Wharton juxtaposes Darrow's adventure with Sophy with his spiritual relationship with Anna as book two shifts the primary focus from Sophy to his pursuit of Anna.

In her youth, Anna's conception of love and marriage was one that focused on a romanticized and idealized version of both (88). This world view governing romance makes her predisposed to desire a soul mate for her ideal match, instead of the coarser physicality that Sophy and Kitty Mayne seek. Yet, she is not completely distanced from the realm of physical love. Darrow had often seen in her, before her marriage, the ability to live a passionate physical love. When they were younger, he thought that her soul was open to experiences which scared her (41). There is a hidden knowledge inside Anna of physical love, yet she refuses to act on that, electing to live in her idealized world instead. She found Darrow intelligent and "liked to hear his voice almost as much as to listen to what he was saying," but that was tainted by the fact that he preferred a physical display of affection to words (92). She did not want his physical attention, but wanted to capture his imagination instead. This passage also echoes the theme found in *The Fruit of the Tree* represented in the reference to Milton. Anna sees herself as Eve who wishes Adam to relate knowledge to her. Anna, however, is still uncertain about the physical side of life. Her preference is to have her Adam relate knowledge to her while proclaiming their eternal, soul love. In essence, she wanted him to acknowledge the greater love of their souls at the expense of the physical love. Given her unfailing insistence on spiritual love, it is not surprising that when she looks back upon her young ideals, she realized that she missed a significant side of life. The world she grew up in was not one of emotion (90). In denying their physical emotions, the world she grew up in was one of a spiritual bond.

The Summers' world was a place where they ignored the physical side of life and taught her to cover the primitive realities of life (91). Anna feels they did not live a physical life, so they needed to find a union elsewhere, on the spiritual plane. The fact that she is aware of this other life implies she will be able to experience it, at some point, with the right person. Both Anna and Darrow assume he is the one to show her the way to this new experience. Darrow believes he can awaken Anna's sexual passion, just as Sophy did for him. He thinks that "he would have put warmth in her veins and light in her eyes: would have made her a woman through and through" (41). Unfortunately for Anna, she removed herself from this world after seeing it in action and the overt display of physicality involving Kitty Mayne. Darrow, not realizing Anna's fear, ultimately believes that "a love like his might have given her the divine gift of self-renewal" (41). He believes that he can awaken her to the knowledge of the love she had missed throughout her life. He would show her the way out of reliving what she had always done and heard to experience life (41). This new life is in the realm beyond the everyday experience, beyond the physical. Once again, the word beyond is tied to a greater love than the characters experience in life, yet this is the first time that beyond is tied to physical love. In linking the concept of beyond to physical love, Wharton is asserting that Darrow sees love for Anna as both physical and spiritual. Looking back at her life as Anna Summers causes the strong belief in a love of souls to take on a "spell of unreality" from which only love can free her (91). The implication is that love of souls at the expense of the physical creates a faux Republic just as much as the love of the physical at the expense of the soul creates a faux Republic. Anna does not have to be on the verge of death in order to receive this love from him, yet she is unable to accept a love that is both physical and spiritual at this point. Instead of receiving his tutoring, Anna runs to the man she believes possessed the imagination to love her soul.

Eventually, she learns that Fraiser's imagination is really a farce. He turned the beauty of the unconventional realm Anna wished to enter into the conventional world she wanted to escape. What she thought was a route to freedom with him was, in fact, a route into greater denial and renunciation. She did know that passion could free her, but the reality of her life gave her no outlet for it (91). Her challenge was either to submit to the lesser world with its denial of passion, the world of Fraiser Leath, or to find "the magic bridge" to the physical love she desired (91). As Anna Summers, she was never able to cross over, but she hoped, in her later life, that Anna Leath would be able to find it and the passion she believed awaited her on the other side. However, by keeping the bridge imagery, Anna implies that she hopes to be able to cross between both worlds.

When Anna first reunites with Darrow, three months before he becomes involved with Sophy, death marks her in the form of widow's clothing, although it is not as strong a mark as the death that surrounded previous characters in Wharton's works. In fact, Darrow's appearance has a profound effect upon her. Upon first seeing him, "her smile had been like a red rose pinned on her widow's mourning" (18). It appears that he has the effect of awakening Anna to the things she had missed in youth. He turns her from the death-marked widow to the woman who is alive with color. Yet, he appreciates her not as a potential physical love at this point but in terms of a "much finer and surer...instrument of expression" just as Guy Thwarte views Nan in *The Buccaneers* (*The Reef* 18). Her mind and spirit, not her physicality are what he discerns about her. In order to keep her soul pure, Darrow convinces himself that Fraiser could never have touched Anna as he could (20). Although she does not speak poorly of Leath, she does not speak of him as her soul mate either.

Even though death marks her, Darrow is surprised to learn that widowhood had not opened her life as he expects (23). She is not free to enter into purely physical love or amorous experiments because she has not given up the idea of finding her soul mate. Instead, she elects to live for her family and delay her entrance into the freedom that others have found in death. He believes that her obstacles were just another sign that she "was still afraid of life" because he only vaguely understands her view of love (41). Anna was not afraid of life, but she was also not going to give up on her dream for a more meaningful love beyond the physical. Although she expected him to help awaken her to the life she had missed, she also hopes to unite on a higher level beyond the physical (92).

Wharton is explicit in demonstrating that Anna does have the potential for experiencing both the physical and spiritual love. Anna, however, is waiting for the right person to awaken her body and soul (89). The thought of Darrow's arrival sets her off on a "flight" of motion and happiness (104). His physical presence allows her to reach a perspective found in many of Wharton's descriptions of the Republic of the Spirit. She felt "herself to be speaking from a far-off airy height, and yet to be wholly gathered into the circle of consciousness which drew its glowing ring about herself and Darrow" (109). Interestingly, she knows that to the world, her words sounded mundane, but to her inner soul, the words expressed the love and beauty only a kindred soul could recognize (109). It is because her words are not expressive of the love that she wishes to share with him that the words were lacking. The soul is waiting to hear the words expressing the love of their souls. Anna's inner self, however, knows that so much can be expressed through physical proximity. She has found her way into the Republic, just by having him near, not through any expressive words as has been the case in the past.

Her belief in the mutual love they share overtakes and subsumes the reality of the love they could have. This idealization is what keeps them apart. When she is her happiest with him, it is when she is in the realm of imagination. If fact, when they are together, she does not only enjoy his physical presence, even though it evokes a physical look of happiness in her. Instead, it is "her imagination [which] flew back and forth, spinning luminous webs of feeling between herself" and Darrow (117). She is much happier to create an imaginary bond between them than to act on any physical love. Her constant delays in their wedding plans are to keep this imaginary love, this spiritual love between them, pure and alive. As soon as their love promises to drop to the earthly realm, Anna wants to withdraw from it. Darrow, however, takes a much more practical view of their love. He finds their shared thoughts and experiences to be "the old delusion" of nature (130). With that one statement, he debunks the notion of a shared language between two like souls and has declared spiritual love to be part of something in which he no longer believes. He analyzes their love in terms of the earthly love. He believes that their like minds are just a way to bring them together for procreation, another way for sexual selection to work. He harbors no romantic notions about their love.

Anna eventually convinces herself that Darrow only wants the spiritual love from her. She is happy in the thought that he wants her as she was, not as she thinks she should be (122). To want her as she was is to want the woman who does not live in life, who knows passion exists, but represses it for a union of souls. However she still does have hope of displaying their love as more than spiritual, because she wanted their souls to stay together in the realm beyond while their bodies were together in reality (124). She is, however, torn between desiring both a physical love and a love of souls. Her youth has taught her that the spiritual love is the ideal because it is a greater union outside of the earthly physicality, but earthly physicality also is part of the life that she would like to experience. In essence, she is seeking a balance between the two.

After their visit to the Temple of Love, a setting that will be revisited in *The Buccaneers*, Darrow decides to relinquish completely the physical love for Anna's dead passion (126). He rationalizes that he could live without passion as long as she loved him (127). He will live her idealized love at the renunciation of his desired love. This rationalization is a relinquishing of his passion to a world of beauty and imagination. In believing this, Darrow often believes that Anna's soul casts a spell over him. He has a feeling of "divine security" when she looks at him because her charm is one of the soul (149). The enchantment creates elements of the faux Republic because he is only seeing half of the love they could share. Although there will be kisses of "promise and communion," Anna no longer only wants the love of souls (127). In fact, the life he envisions after their marriage is in direct opposition to Anna's dreams. Whereas she is hoping for an awakening into total love of both physical and spiritual union, Darrow dreams of withdrawing from the physical and living in the spiritual. Darrow has lived out his passionate experiments with Sophy, who found the primacy of physical to be the height of love for her. Sophy, much like her sister and Jimmy Brance, has realized the pleasure and satisfaction in a physical love. Darrow has had his fill of the physical and is ready to settle down to a love with his soul mate. Anna, as Anna Summers, has lived a life aware of secret beauty, a life afraid of physical love, is finally ready to experience a balanced love with her soul mate.

Just when they have convinced themselves that they are happy in their love, Sophy reappears. Darrow immediately notes a change in her physical characteristics. Although she looks less alive, it takes the light on her face to bring out a "whiteness" in her that "startled him" (144). Sophy is taking on the physical characteristics of a dead or dying woman. She is losing her liveliness and becoming pale, yet that is not in line with the life he had envisioned for her. In Darrow's mind, she was happy with their physical love and wanted nothing more from him than that. Her fate, it seems, is heading along the path of Wharton's other beautiful women. It is unclear whether this new look for Sophy is a result of fear at Darrow's response or a result of Owen's love for her. Yet, she was able to remain alive and vivacious during her experiment with Darrow even though she knew he would never find her to be his soul mate. Her relationship with Owen, however, is not the physical experiment she had with Darrow. Owen's believing that she is his soul mate, it appears, is turning her into a dead-like or dying soul mate.

Darrow's desire regarding Sophy is still to assist to her (146). In their time alone, she begins to revive the physical love that Darrow had relinquished with Anna. Her presence starts to reawaken emotions he buried during his time with Anna (147). He awakens to the world of the physical again. From this point on, Darrow is torn between his duties to both romantic relationships. He believes Anna promises him security and deep communion on a spiritual level, whereas Sophy promises him life and physical love. Interestingly, Darrow never sees it as a choice between two women he loves. In fact, he often tells himself that Sophy means nothing to him. Yet, Sophy's arrival forces Darrow to cut back, perhaps unconsciously, on his physical affection toward Anna. Anna, however, is sensitive enough to notice the change. She realizes that Darrow is too preoccupied with something to kiss her when they are alone. Anna just does not have the full view of the situation to understand why there is this change at this moment, but she is perceptive enough to notice the change. For Darrow, there is never a question about his feelings towards the women. He is in love with Anna. He has total faith in her loving him (197). He would never consider giving up her love, even if it means relinquishing his physical adventures of the past. He defines himself in terms of Anna's love and devotion. Without her love, he would be nothing. Their love protects them from the world he thinks Anna fears.

After they announce the marriages, Sophy begins to fade from his world. Her beauty returns, as does the dress she wore at the theater in Paris. Yet, just at the point where both couples should be their happiest, Sophy wants to abandon it all. She does not want to marry a man who would force her to become the pale woman she was when Darrow first saw her at the Leath's home. Once the news of Darrow's adventure with Sophy reaches Anna, he sees an incredible change in Sophy toward death. She feels she has inflicted incredible pain upon the man she loved. Knowing their physical love would always be between them, Sophy feels she must remove herself from the periphery of his life. Instead of wishing for a change, Sophy refuses to forget their time together because remembering is her way of keeping him close (242). She will keep him and their adventure to herself, but she will not let it fade into the death and darkness. Sophy will keep their physical love to herself (293).

It is only when Darrow tries to convince her to stay with Owen that Sophy confesses her feelings regarding their time together in Paris. She tried to look at the situation as Darrow did, but was unsuccessful. However, in realizing this, she also learned that she took more away from their time together than he ever could. She not only risked her reputation and future happiness, but she also risked her heart by falling in love with Darrow, allowing herself to love him beyond the physical into the spiritual realm. It appears that he has unwittingly taught her that there is a love beyond the physical love, a love that heightens and complements the physical. She is able to love Darrow in a way he had not imagined. Her confession forces him to reconsider his role in the adventure. Although he had not meant to touch her so deeply, he questions his later actions (243). Eventually, during their time together, kisses replaced words (244). This deep physical connection is the reverse of the spiritual connection which substitutes speech for the kiss. In thinking that the physical was their only way of connecting, he reduces her to the primitive elemental passions so as to convince himself of his innocence in their adventure.

Darrow's view of their life changes once Anna realizes the adventure that took place between Sophy and Darrow. When he looks at himself in the mirror, all he can see was Sophy's love written on his face (250-251). Gauging one's love in the mirror will appear again in *Summer* and *The Glimpses of the Moon*. Darrow, however, still has not come to terms with his role in their adventure and sees Sophy as the passionate being. There is no mention of the possibility of Anna's passion erasing Sophy's because that is not the love he desires from her. That is not the spell he believes she casts.

Anna's confronting the totality of Darrow's passion forces her to rethink their relationship. She believes "she had seemed to look into the very ruins of his soul…and she had been looking at two sides of the same thing, and the side she had seen had been all light and life, and his a place of graves" (254–255). The difference in their views of love, she now knows, is due to the fact that they were looking at two different kinds of love. Anna has lived the majority of her life believing that a love with one's soul mate was the ultimate goal. Darrow, however, has lived a different life. He has known the pleasure of physical love. He also believes that Anna can awaken to a physical love with the proper guide. Yet, he does not know how to guide her to this greater understanding. Anna, however, sees his physical adventures as a corrupting influence since they were not experienced with her. Once he has returned to her side, he begins to deny the physical side as she had demanded him to do earlier in their relationship just as she wishes to awaken to it. Anna blames her unhappiness on the fact that she had finally tried to step away from the spiritual love with Darrow and move into the physical side of love. Much like her attitude toward their love, she tries to keep her pain an idealized, romanticized pain. Her pain is something for her alone (265). She feels that although she is suffering, she is the only one with a right to suffer.

Darrow's relationship with Sophy has tainted the idealized notion Anna had of their love. Her only solution to recoup an idealized world is to push Darrow away and surrender to her idealized misery and suffering. Eventually, she is torn between the desire to ignore his relationship with Sophy and the desire to know all about their adventure. This position is the one Anna has been in her entire life. She is at a turning point at which she can return to the world which denied its passion, or embrace the world that she has always envied, the world of physical love.

Her first instinct is to return to "a kind of torpor, a deadness of soul traversed by wild flashes of pain" (276). This description hearkens back to the woman's death in "The Fullness of Life." Anna, however, has a different perspective in that she feels that although her life is over, she can retain the idealized image of Darrow. In this state, she thinks she can separate the real Darrow from her idealized version of him (277). She feels she could separate the same two parts of him, much as she has separated these two parts of her life. However, she does come to the understanding that he was comprised of both parts (277), just as the two types of love in her life were both part of her. She still believes that the idealized love of the soul is the ideal, ultimate union, but she also comes to realize that she needs to acknowledge physical love. With this realization, Anna takes a step toward a fuller conception of love which is nearly balanced. However, she still desires the spiritual love to be in place before the physical love.

Interestingly, Anna cannot relinquish her longing for love between souls. She believes "there *was* such a love as she had dreamed, and she meant to go on believing in it, and cherishing the thought that she was worthy of it" (280). Whatever comes between her and that spiritual love sickens her (280). Perhaps the most appalling element of this love triangle for Anna is that upon learning from Sophy that Darrow had always and only loved Anna, she became aware that Sophy embraced a deeper and more fulfilling passion than Anna has ever imagined (284). Sophy possesses a passion that Anna never had and never will have in her ability to see the depth of Darrow's love for Anna. She feels she must give him up completely because of this. Just as she comes to terms with her not being able to keep Darrow, he appeals to her desire for both kinds of love; he tells her that eventually she will understand the events. That she "will some day [understand it all]: [she was] made to feel everything" (289). She had desired the ability to feel both the spiritual and the physical love throughout her entire life, and it appears that Darrow has understood this about her. Finally, she recognizes "sensations so separate from her romantic thoughts of him that she saw her body and soul divided against themselves" (290). Her new knowledge comes at a price of acknowledging a separation between body and soul, physical and spiritual. With this battle raging inside of her, she feels that she could not lose him. She finally has confronted the passions which her earlier life denied her. Her spirit and body are at war, but also open to new experiences. For Anna, this new self emerging out of the conflict does not end in unqualified passion and happiness. She realizes that she will always have questions about her love's true feelings despite the fact that she feels he knows her thoughts. The conflict between physical love and the love of souls is not resolved by the end of the novel, just as Anna's decision regarding Darrow is left unresolved. Perhaps, these feelings regarding love are just as unresolved in Wharton's mind at this point in her life as they are in Anna's.

There are hints, however, of the direction the future will take for Anna and for Wharton herself. While Anna is caught in an infinite oscillation between belonging to Darrow body and soul and wanting him completely out of her life, one can imagine Sophy's life being fuller from the experience. She returns to her original situation, but with the knowledge that she had loved Darrow and had felt a strong passion for him. When they are together in the forest, she wanted him to speak a word to free her (301). Anna's imagination, however, could not release the though of Darrow's time and passion with Sophy. She feels she could begin to understand the need for physical love. Anna even feels released when she tells Darrow she wants "to know everything" (326). By ending the novel on the name of Jimmy Brance, Wharton hints that the focus should be primarily on physical love from this point forward. There is, it appears, no prominent place for a romantic spiritual love in the world found in *The Reef* and in Wharton's world. This is in direct contrast to her earlier works, which upheld the notion of spiritual love being the ultimate goal of love and the physical being a lesser influence. With this change toward the primacy of the physical, the death-like lover begins to fade into the background. Although there are some brief hints of death imagery, the lovers in these middle works are, for the most part, alive and lovely. Only when they deny their physical side do they start to take on the death-like appearance. The primacy of the physical love becomes more explicit in the next novel, *Summer*, where Charity's first encounter with love is physical and she must devise her concept of a soul mate only after knowledge of physical love.

CHAPTER SEVEN

Summer

Wharton was aware that *Summer* was different from, yet similar to, her other works, as revealed in a letter to Gaillard Lapsley in which she refers to it as "hot Ethan" (Lewis and Lewis 385). This reference confirms the idea that Wharton felt *Summer* was a companion piece to the earlier, extremely darker world of *Ethan Frome*. It also shows that she is aware of the change in her work from the winter world of *Ethan Frome* to the warm passion of *Summer*. It was a more passionate version of *Ethan Frome* not only in terms of landscape and increased overt sexuality, but also in that physical love is no longer seen as a negative linked to death.

Yet, this novel becomes increasingly problematic for readers due to the prominence of an implied incestuous relationship between Royall and Charity. It is interesting to note that this implied incest did not concern earlier reviewers (Benstock 328), but the concern seems to be a product of minds of more recent eras. Perhaps some of the discomfort regarding Wharton's use of the undercurrent of incest in this work stems from the fact that Wharton revises her notion of love and death in this work not only by giving her heroine a chance to experience physically satisfying love and spiritual companionship in life, but also by concluding with a picture of qualified happiness.

Prior to meeting Harney, Charity has not had much experience with love and romance. Being from a small town which stresses the negative aspects of physical love and people who are not interested in the books surrounding her allow for Charity to be a relatively blank slate regarding idealized notions of love. What she does know, however, is physical love and its potential for destruction when motivated by loneliness. She was the recipient of Royall's misplaced physical advances, which he later regretted making, and is the gatekeeper of the library where young town-folk meet their lovers (75). She is also aware of the fact that indulging in physical love results in having to leave town as is the case with Julia Hawes. Yet, she has neither met her soul mate nor given the concept much thought. When her story opens, she cannot even articulate what her ideal soul mate is. She finds Royall distasteful because he desires physical love, even though they share a common bond of loneliness. However, he is the only suitable male influence in her life, but even he has failed to educate her in non-physical love. In not legally adopting her, he does not create the parental bond and the feeling of paternal love. Instead, the situation constantly reminds Charity that she is a living example of his charity, neither a child he loves, nor the product of love. Denying Charity the love of a family and, more specifically fatherly love, serves to distance her from the town. Royall's failure to bring her into the love of the family ensures that "she felt no particular affection for him" even though she knew his secrets and the extent of his loneliness (13). These are the views of love that Charity has known. Her guardian does not love her like a daughter, yet wanted to experience a physical love with her that will force her to be expelled from the only life she has known. What Charity does not yet realize is that Royall actually desires much more from her than just a physical love, he desires a balance of the physical and spiritual loves with her.

Although she refuses Royall's physical pursuit of her, she does realize that he has some effect on her. It is his "deep voice that sometimes moved her," but it does not move her beyond being astonished at his being able to reach her (16). She was not expecting him to be able to touch her at any point in her life, and more importantly, not at this time. The fact that he can reach her at a time when she most obviously wants to refuse him confuses her. Her strong attraction to his voice, however, lasts through the novel. As mentioned earlier, song is a key trait in selecting a mate according to Darwin. In this case, Royall's song is his voice. The pull of his voice will be demonstrated again later in his speech during the Old Home Week festivities. This attraction is one of the signs that they have a deeper connection than she is willing to acknowledge. As we shall see with Harney, it is a shared language, along with his physical touch, that eventually defines Charity's version of the Republic of the Spirit. Although Charity does not think of Royall in terms of the Republic at this point, her attraction to his voice foreshadows the qualified happiness upon which the novel ends. It is interesting to note that Charity's way of punishing Royall after his attempted physical relationship with her is to withhold speech from him (18). Upon resuming their verbal connection, he proposes. It is not the proposal which offends her, but his physical appearance. She no longer knows how to classify Royall since he is neither physically attractive to her, nor the guardian which she has come to know him. Instead, he looks "like a hideous parody of the fatherly old man she had always known" (19). In fact, her rejection of him is on a physical basis, both the way he looked physically and his physical desire. Her hiring Verena serves as much to humiliate him as it does to remind him that she does not desire a physical love from him. She hopes that her deaf assistant will remind him that Verena would neither know the depth of his loneliness nor fall for the thrill of his voice. His voice cannot touch Verena so they would never have the potential for a deeper bond.

From the moment Lucius Harney enters North Dormer, his role in awakening Charity to love is made abundantly clear. When she first sees him on the street, she retreated into the Royall's house, examined her appearance in the mirror, only to find her appearance somewhat lacking (2). Drawing upon sexual selection, Charity feels that if she just had one different physical "ornamentation" she would be desirable and complete. Since the trait she elects to focus upon cannot be changed, she projects her frustration about her lack on the town and that makes her "hate everything" about her current life (2). If only she could see herself as desirable by someone she deems worthy, she would not be in a position where everything is distasteful. Annabel Balch is her ideal beauty at this moment and Charity feels she will never be beautiful enough to attract a man in comparison to her. Perhaps a bit more subtle of a connection is that Charity's desire for Annabel's eyes could be her desire for a love of the soul, since the eyes have often been linked to the soul. Yet, it is the physical element which brings Charity to contemplate a love of the soul. It is interesting that she selects Annabel as the idealized beauty as they have had little direct interaction with each other. Yet, the only other beauty in town was Julia Hawes, a disgraced woman. Therefore, Annabel, a visitor from another town, who the town does not know well enough to gossip about, and who would never degrade herself with a boy from North Dormer, becomes Charity's ideal to emulate. In secretly selecting to be like Annabel, Charity shows that she could be receptive to a love of the soul through a physical love. What Charity does not know quite yet is that the woman she compares herself to is also her primary competition for Harney's love.

Wharton further emphasizes Charity and Harney's physical relationship by having Harney fall speechless upon seeing her. Eventually, for Charity, "everything that had followed seemed to have grown out of that look: his way of speaking to her, his quickness at catching her meaning" (48). These incidents serve to set the early tone of their relationship as a physical love instead of a union of souls. They build their physical love surrounded by an aura of death at the library, where they first meet, the deadest place in town. Charity even questions whether Honorious Hatchard "felt any deader in his grave than she did in his library" (5). By thinking this, she places herself as on equal footing, or perhaps even graver footing, with the dead. The library has been dead for some time. It is a place that neither receives new books nor loans out the old ones (3). The library is a forgotten place. There is no new, fresh breath of air for the building or the knowledge contained within it. To further the image of the library as a "ridiculous mausoleum" (31), the worms are the only ones devouring the books, the knowledge, contained within its walls (7). Nevertheless, in this deathly setting, the first strands of their passionate relationship begin to flower. Yet, the aura of death is much milder than that found in the previous works discussed.

Harney's interest in Charity's beauty has a reverse effect than we have seen in the works previously discussed. Instead of his interest causing her to look decimated and deathly, "her small face, usually so darkly pale, glowed like a rose in the faint orb of light" (23). She begins to see herself as physically desirable in the way she imagines people find Annabel Balch desirable. In demonstrating this, Wharton shows that death is no longer a primary element in finding love. While observing her physical change, Charity indulges in her first fantasy regarding marriage. Her nightgown becomes the wedding dress she wears walking down the aisle to meet her lover, Harney. That the "unbleached night-gown" replaces the idealized virginal white wedding dress further links Charity's and Harney's relationship to the bedroom (23). Strangely enough, once her relationship turns sexual, she no longer desires the image of herself married to Harney. Instead, she wonders who he will marry. Since the imagination is the way to the Republic of the Spirit, it is interesting to note that Charity's imagination finds a place for Harney without her. In doing this, she shows that she knows, perhaps subconsciously, that he is not the ideal mate for her. However, she will need him to awaken her to physical love before finding a love of souls with another.

Their verbal misunderstandings further illustrate the purely physical nature of their relationship. While she retreats to the hills and "lay immersed in an inarticulate well-being" (11), Harney speaks to his aunt to inadvertently get her fired from her job, the only thing that mattered to her. His verbal deception, as it were, arouses her anger with him. She felt betrayed by Harney not only for his verbal mishaps, but also for his not kissing her, for not taking physical advantage of her. In betraying her verbally, by not joining her in inarticulate, but shared language, he took advantage of their potential soul union, not her body. She was expecting him to take physical liberties based upon the conversation of the girls in her class regarding boys. Although the verbal deception hurts her feelings, their failure to obtain a physical closeness hurts more. This sort of verbal mishap appears throughout their relationship and serves to distance them from any hope of a soul union of like minds.

While Charity and Harney are having these verbal gaffs, Royall and Charity forge a stronger verbal connection. He is the one who tells her of Harney's deception regarding her job at the library. Harney's appearance also makes Charity finally see Royall though she had previously ignored him. Before Harney, he had just been a figure in the shadows of her life, much as Sophy was to Darrow in *The Reef*. Once Harney has contact with Royall, she realizes that Royall "was probably poorer than people knew" but that he was also better than everyone else in the town (44). Also of note is that Charity's impression of Royall's verbal skills increases in Harney's presence. She believed his speech improved "now that he had a listener who understood him" in Harney (44). Royall is, essentially, misunderstood by both Charity and the town. Yet, once he has a person who is willing and able to understand him, Royall's strength and power grow.

Once Harney awakens Charity to physical love, her interest in the Mountain becomes more prevalent. Before his arrival, the town had embedded in her the sense that the Mountain was a place of unruly promiscuity and wickedness, even though it was her home. In her time with Royall, the Mountain became a constant threat used to bring her back under Royall's control. In Harney's eyes, the stigma of the Mountain fades. Charity adopts his view that the Mountain was "a little independent kingdom...[of] rough customers; but they must have a good deal of character" (41). It is after learning that Harney admired that community that she claims her connection to the Mountain community. Royall, however, attempts to use her

Mountain heritage to humiliate her when he tells Harney the story of her birth and coming to live with him. Interestingly, she is not upset by the fact that she is from the Mountain, but because her parents sent her away from the Mountain community. The Mountain's mixed status turns it into "a kind of actualized, corrupted [R]epublic of the [S]pirit" (Papke 131).

Instead of believing the Mountain as a "corrupted" Republic, I would argue that it is a faux Republic along the lines of the enchanted forests in earlier works. Claiming the Mountain is corrupted, denies Wharton's positive view of the primacy of physical love found throughout the novella. In fact, much like in *The Reef*, the Republic of the Spirit takes a lesser role to a physical love. The faux Republic of the Mountain is certainly not the realm of finer air of the world beyond, yet it does have its own appeal. Although the town is certain that the Mountain was bad, Charity was not so quick to judge them (4). In the eyes of young Harney, and later Charity, the Mountain is not corrupted because the inhabitants form their own world that does not believe in the judgments of others (41). In branding the Mountain in this way, Harney creates a fantasy about Charity's origins. However, having descended from this faux Republic makes Charity feel that the distance between herself and Harney is too great for them to overcome (47). She realizes that Harney sees the Mountain as a romanticized ideal and not the bad place the town views it to be, but as a kingdom of physical love. In her prior rejection of her connection to the Mountain, she had rejected physical love. With Harney's guidance, however, she comes to claim the physical. The notion of the independent kingdom recalls Justine Brent's desire for an inner kingdom in *The Fruit of the Tree*. In noticing the physical kingdom and desiring the soul of a lady in Annabel, Harney could be desiring both a physical love and love of souls. However, he feels he cannot find both in one woman.

As Harney takes precedence in Charity's life, Royall becomes less important to her (58). The only way he can return to Charity's reality is to assert his physical presence by banishing Harney from the house. With Harney's eviction, Charity feels as if her dreams were no longer within her reach (49). The recurring imagery of drowning at the loss of the physical love was also present in *Ethan Frome* and "The Fullness of Life." It is this physical assertion which causes Charity to flee to Harney's side. Despite Royall's forcing her to flee to Harney and Harney's attempts to equate her with the physical, she is not as eager to take the final step into a life of sexual freedom. When she seeks him in his room at night, she refuses to make contact because she finally understood that a meeting would lead to a sexual encounter. It is the event that Charity has only a vague understanding of in theory, but not in actual practice. It was, in a phrase, physical passion. She is, in essence, still an innocent girl, even more innocent than some of the town girls, despite her mountain heritage. Although she was not afraid of physical passion, she did not want to degrade herself in his eyes (68). She did not want to reach the vulgar level of some of the other town girls. Interestingly, although she does not openly state it, her desire not to lower herself also shows that she is seeking something more than a physical love. She will not be happy with just a physical love at this point, but she does not have the knowledge of what other kinds of love could be available to her as evidenced by her desire for Annabel's eyes.

It is because of this lack of desire to become less of a lady that Charity responds more to Harney's words of "simple friendship" than his desire for a physical connection with her (84). The bond of camaraderie if often an element we have seen connected with the Republic, ranging from Lily's first appeal to Selden to Nan St. George's appeal to Guy Thwarte in *The Buccaneers*. This belief in their friendship also allows her to believe they share "a private language" found in the silence they share in other people's company (84). This shared language is similar to what other heroines in Wharton's works sought with their soul mates. While Charity bases her new concept of love on the notion of friendship with Harney, she also believes that this friendship will keep them from marrying. She believes he wants and needs a love she is unwilling to provide him at this point. Once he kisses her, however, a whole new perspective opens to her. She realizes that "an unknown Harney…revealed himself" in this kiss (98). This new version of Harney reflects elements of traits for successful sexual selection. He was "a Harney who dominated her, and yet over whom she felt herself possessed of a new mysterious power" (98). In allowing his physical love to overwhelm her, she also became aware of her new control over him and other men. She is awakening to physical love. Just as Lily's power over Selden and Ethan's power over Mattie evolved in the faux Republic, where the physical takes precedence, Charity's awakening to power and domination is through physical love.

Charity's awakening is, to some extent, what Royall feared would happen under Harney's tutelage. However, Royall's knowledge and concern regarding her relationship with Harney evokes her hatred. He tries to reach her on the verbal level, by having her explain her side of the story which is the subject of town gossip, but she refuses. Her refusal forces him to draw a direct comparison between the love he is offering Charity and the love Harney is offering her. As Royall sees it, "if he'd wanted you the right way, he'd have said so" (75). He knows that Harney has no intention of forming anything other than an amorous experiment with her. It is at this point that Royall declares to Charity that he had always loved her (75). Despite the one lapse, he has loved her with a fuller love than anyone has offered her. This, it seems, explains why he never adopted her, which would have created a father-daughter bond and forbidden their marriage. Instead, he loved her on a deeper, soul level along with a physical love. As if to prove his decent intentions, he proposes again and offers her an escape from North Dormer. Yet, his words did not reach her heart because she has been awakened to a physical love with Harney that she had rejected earlier with Royall. She has not fully awakened to the love Royall can provide. It is interesting to note that although she thinks of words to harm him, she does not use them against him. Although she is not ready to love him, she no longer wishes to hurt him.

It is in the presence of the new Harney that she becomes, as Royall calls her at the Independence Day celebration, a "damn-bare-headed whore" (101). This experience is significant to Charity not only because she becomes lessened in Royall's eyes, but in many ways, Royall is fallen in Charity's eyes. Although Charity knew of his drinking, she did not know he was a member of the society which included the infamous town prostitute, Julia Hawes. In Charity's mind, being seen in public with Julia and her companions disgraces him (100). In being seen with these people, he once again forces her to see that he is aware of the physical love that others experience. He does not want to be solely relegated to the world of spirit, but would like a balance between the physical love and a love of souls with the right woman. Her first instinct, to assert her control over him through verbal demands, fails miserably. They become, at this point, equally fallen in each other's eyes. Upon returning home, Charity feels that she is looking "from the other side of the grave" (103) in the same way that Anna felt looking at Darrow after learning of his experiment with Sophy. Royall's stepping out beyond her accepted definition of him causes her to withhold speech from him once again. They believe they are now equals concerning physical love.

Royall, however, was a bit premature in asserting the completeness of Charity's physical love for Harney. It is only upon learning that she plans to flee to the Mountain after Royall's treatment of her at the celebration that she and Harney take the final step into a physical union. Once he realizes she is serious about leaving, he stops "listening to her, he was only looking at her, with the passionate absorbed expression she had seen in his eyes after they had kissed...He was the new Harney again, the Harney abruptly revealed in that embrace" (108). He finally gives his physical love full reign to express itself. The new Harney appears just as he believes her return to the Mountain means a return to the physical love the town feels the Mountain represents. What he does not understand is that she wants to flee from the totality of love. When she does finally leave, and he tracks her down, he seems to understand her needs. His kiss upon finding her is not to express physical love, but is a friendly kiss (109). Yet, that feeling does not last long. Whereas Charity thinks Royall wants her to be a fallen woman like Julia, she becomes convinced that Harney wants her to be a lady. However, she is mistaken. It is Harney, not Royall, who wants her to be the sexually free woman like Julia.

After their first sexual encounter, "all her tossing contradictory impulses were merged in a fatalistic acceptance of his will" (116). She loses her independence and selfhood in this new physical love with Harney. Just the sound of his name puts her in a dream-like state. Yet, she is merely one adventure among many to Harney, just as she is just one girl among many girls who occupy his bedroom during Old Home Week. Interestingly, just as Charity becomes one girl among many in Harney's bedroom, Royall takes center stage, both literally and figuratively during the Old Home Week festivities. Although she is still angry with him and withholding her speech from him, his song is able to touch her. His speech, urging people to come to North Dormer "for *good*...and not for bad...or just for indifference" (128) causes her to listen, once again, to the "rolling music of his voice" (129). She begins to see the "light of response" in his listeners' faces and, for a moment, is able to see the power that he has (128). Yet, it is not enough to keep her from seeking out Harney in the audience. Given Wharton's interest in Plato, Royall's beckoning people to find goodness in the town, could also be his way of appealing to the soul's love for the "permanent possession of goodness" (*Symposium* 49).

Charity tries to find a soul love in Harney, along with their physical love. Suddenly, it is not just Harney's kisses which she loved, but also his words

(120). Given that the one thing she did like about Royall was listening to him talk, it appears that she is trying to replace Royall with Harney. However, Charity feels the effects of the faux Republic after their sexual encounter. Harney "had caught her up and carried her away into a new world" (121). She thinks they have reached a new understanding, where nothing mattered, except their physical love. She felt that "under his touch things deep down in her struggled to the light and sprang up like flowers in the sunshine" (122). His touch is the element which brings her to the faux Republic, to the Mountain, and she realizes she should not be ashamed of their physical love. The love depicted in this novel is a positive flowering brought to light while the absence of the lover makes one feel ghost-like, death-like. No longer does the lover have to be death-like to be worthy of love. Instead, she must be full of light and life, just like Mattie Silver and Sophy Viner.

With the physical love taking prominence in these middle novels, there is an emphasis on the faux Republic because the faux Republic focuses on the love of the physical, rather than the love of one soul for another. Charity's and Harney's kiss occurs after their visit to the brown house in Porcupine, surrounded by a death-like landscape. Weeds, nettles and a "poisonous" garden surround the house, yet they feel close to each other in this place (52). Even the home they make for themselves is desolate. It was "bleached to a ghostly grey...The garden palings had fallen, but the broken gate dangled between its posts, and the path to the house was marked by rose-bushes run wild...[T]he house was as dry and pure as the interior of a long-empty shell" (110). Since the emphasis is on the physical nature of their relationship, the idealized love becomes a physical love, not a spiritual love.

Eventually, Royall intrudes into their bliss, forcing the thought of marriage to intrude along with him. Marriage was not what Harney and Charity had intended for their relationship. The cares of the town were not to bother them in their house of love. When the thought of marriage enters their world, Harney's "voice seemed like a stranger's" (140). He is no longer close to her, but farther away than he had ever been. The values of the town have intruded in their Mountain retreat, just when Charity and Harney were forging the ties of a similar language. She tries to answer him, but finds that she is speechless (140). Neither truly wants to confront this new element imposed on them, pulling them farther away from the Mountain ideal they desire. Interestingly, it is only once Harney writes to her that she realizes that a "spell bound her to him" that could not be severed (142). It is only the thought of marriage that forces her to realize the "spell" and acknowledge that it cannot last. When she finally does write, it is not an expression of her love, but to set him free.

Although her relationship with Harney has ended, Royall is still in her life. Like a knight in shining armor, Royall, once again, arrives to escort this new Charity down the Mountain. This time, however, his actions create "a softness at her heart" that had happened only once previously (177). The Charity born out of the aura of death is a more understanding and receptive woman than she had been in the past. Although her actions appear mostly passive, "she began to feel like living again" (179). Yet, it is a different life she will be living. She will no longer fall victim to the great heights of physical and spiritual love, but will have a more balanced version of love.

This change in perception makes her see the world in a wider scope. Instead of refusing Royall's proposal because she hates him or finds him distasteful, she wishes to reject him because she was not entitled to accept the proposal while pregnant with another man's child (180). She knows the town will attach a stigma to Royall's reputation if he marries her, and she does not want to bring that shame upon him. However, his voice penetrates her thoughts. It is his voice from which she draws strength and comfort. His voice is what finally convinces her to accept him (180). He no longer is someone she hates and rejects. He becomes a strong voice and presence in her life. She learns that she can draw strength and life from him in a way she never thought she could. During their drive into town, she even is able to feel that, at times, she "seemed to be sitting beside her lover with the leafy arch of summer bending over them" (182). She is, on one level, revising her opinion of Royall. She is awakening to the man he really is.

The wedding and honeymoon, if it can be called a honeymoon, end on a qualified and quiet happiness. Although many scholars find this to be an unhappy ending, it is not as unhappy as endings in Wharton's previous works (Erlich 126, Papke 132, Pfeiffer 157, Waid xiv). There is hope that their life together will be something into which they can grow. She does not want to dwell on the life she had with Harney. Although her wedding ring is too big for her finger, it implies that there is room for them to grow into their marriage, to, perhaps, a love for each other. In fact, this is better than having a ring that is too tight, implying a suffocating and restricting marriage. That both Royall and Charity can change and grow is prevalent throughout the novel and emphasized by Royall doing all he can to clean up and become the man she desires by their wedding day. Her last twinge of terror is over the wedding night, but that too is resolved as he does not push for a sexual relationship, but elects to sleep on the chair, watching over her.

In the end, Charity realizes she will be safe and protected with Royall. Although the relationship may not be perfect or any romantic ideal, it is the closest thing to a happy ending available to her. The most intriguing thing to note is that before returning to North Dormer, Royall and Charity proclaim the "goodness" of each other. The choice of the word "good" evokes Royall's speech from Old Home Week. Thus, they are returning to North Dormer not for other reasons, but for the "good" he prescribed in his speech. Although they may not be in the ideal, romantic relationship, they will be good for each other and the town. However, perhaps they can eventually also find a love of souls.

Throughout *Summer*, Wharton presents a picture of an uneasy acceptance of the physical love she found as an inferior love in earlier works. Much as in *The Reef*, she presents a character who is torn between the two types of love, but *Summer* expands on the notion of the physical love. Finally, there is an element of happiness and fulfillment being found in a physical love that, in the past, was found only in the spiritual love. Although Charity discovers Eros with Harney, it is a fragile form of love that outsiders can destroy. It is only after a figurative death, when she lies in the bed recently vacated by her dead mother that Charity comes to terms with a fuller form of love which is built upon being with someone for the good of the body and the soul.

CHAPTER EIGHT

The Glimpses of the Moon

At first glance, Wharton presents love in *The Glimpses of the Moon* as being founded upon business and economics, more so than in any of her previous works. As the story of two people, seemingly setting such a high importance on making good matches that they marry each other for the gifts they will receive and to make themselves "new" to their friends again, it also seems the strangest place to find characters achieving a more balanced version of love attained on earth. In essence, this novel is a story about finding a balanced love between two equal partners. Unlike her previous works, this novel begins with the death of love and ends with the characters finding the truth about their love and each other. Death and death-like imagery play a lesser role in this novel, which reveals a greater acceptance of the characters finding and fighting for their happiness on earth. This change is possible because Wharton has more faith in physical love than spiritual love at this point.

Wharton uses this novel to depict a more realistic notion of love. Nick Lansing and Susy Branch's story begins not with a courtship or even a desire to enter the Republic of the Spirit, but with the couple already living in their Republic. They have the "imagination" to create such a special place (7, 13). Yet, Susy did not expect a deeper bond beyond the friendship they shared (7). Although Nick and Susy envision their marriage as an experiment, a word normally applied to brief physical entanglements, their honeymoon at Como has elements of the Republic. The two are secluded away from outside influences; they are beyond care and have an understanding and connection that flows between them. In fact, as Killoran points out, their Republic begins with Nick's marriage proposal up on the hill. Since they actually go through with the marriage, their continued bond reveals that they have entered into the Republic.

Interestingly, their entrance into this realm is initially based upon thinking of love not as a romantic ideal, but as a business transaction. Neither has noticed they are soul mates, because they are more concerned with the physical rewards instead of love of a soul mate in marriage. Despite entering into the Republic on these terms, they are blissfully happy together. In portraying this, Wharton has subtly changed her depiction of the Republic. The characters are unaware of the deeper union they have with each other until they have separated. Instead, it is their physical connection balanced with their spiritual camaraderie that allows them to enter into happiness. This balance reveals a more attainable view of love, yet, as we shall see, there is still some lingering desire for an idealized soul love. It is only when Nick and Susy are equals that they can acknowledge their love for each other.

Although Nick and Susy begin their trial marriage believing that it is purely a business deal, they are deluding themselves (13). It is during a visit to the Fulmers, who were an example of what happens when people marry for love, which their plan begins to take root (16). The Fulmers were poor. They did not advance in material possessions through marriage. They were what Nick and Susy, along with various other couples we have discussed, could become if they married for love instead of as a business deal. In essence, they did the very thing that society warns against. If Nick and Susy's marriage was based on true love, they would end up struggling like Grace and Nat. That is not the life they want. Nick and Susy do not realize, at this point, that the shared love between soul mates is worth the struggle. In spite of these perceived flaws in their relationship, Nat and Grace were better when together (16). Their marriage, it seems, has enhanced both their souls and their bodies. The fact that Nat and Grace are improved in a situation where their friends believe they should be miserable sends Nick and Susy to the forest to plot their marriage experiment. So, just as the Fulmers served as an example before Nick and Susy acknowledge their love for each other, the Fulmers also serve as an expression of an ideal love, as we shall see later.

Although Nick and Susy are skeptical regarding the longevity of Nat and Grace's relationship, it is while they are in the forest overlooking the house that they agree to this game of marriage. This scene resembles other scenes in which the characters invoked the Republic of the Spirit. They are high above the world, looking down upon it, creating a world and a feeling all their own. While in this setting, they devise a marriage in which they could be with each other. She does not want a marriage where one person must be above another, but a marriage that is between equals. It is only in the rarer air, high above the Fulmers' house that she is able to conceive of this sort of match with Nick. The match they design will be materially advantageous, since they will be living off of others for at least a year, but potentially not truly happy, since it is built upon a business transaction, rather than love. Interestingly, Nick has half of what Susy was looking for in her ideal version of a mate. Although he appears unable to provide her with enormous wealth because he is an author, he does provide her with the bond of camaraderie (8). For Nick, as for Susy, there is "a kind of free-masonry" of ideas which made his friendship with her complete (15). Their "free-masonry of ideas" draws upon the principles of brotherhood and mutual aid, the founding principles of The Order of Free-Masons. These principles are present in Nick's and Susy's relationship in their desire to help the other to a more prosperous match. They have a strong bond. Yet, they take their feelings for each other for granted. Although their friends know about the marriage's foundations, they also believe that Nick and Susy belong together. Nick and Susy, however, cannot see that they were destined for each other's love.

Given the shaky foundation of their beginning, it is somewhat surprising that Wharton emphasizes the spiritual nature of their relationship. In fact, Susy's ability to manage their physical needs is detrimental to their happiness. While they are in their Republic at Como, they do appear to be the idealized, blissful romantic couple (3). Only their material rewards mar the "magic carpet" provided by the moon, their "tutelary orb" (3). Having the moon as their guide is a bit of a mixed blessing. As Barbara G. Walker points out, the moon has many associations, some positive and some negative. Many of these can apply to the Lansing's relationship. For example, the Romans believed that the moon was linked to pure souls (Walker 671). If this was the meaning intended by Wharton, then the glimpses of the moon could be a commentary on the state of Nick's and Susy's souls. Most likely, Wharton hoped to connect the cyclical nature of the moon with the cyclical nature of Nick and Susy's relationship. When they see the full moon they are experiencing the heights of love. This would also tie in to connecting the moon to magic (Walker 673) and the view of the moon as the house of souls (671). When they glimpse the moon at its fullest, Nick and Susy glimpse a magical love encompassing their souls. As the moon fades from their lives, they can no longer see or believe in that magical love which joins their souls. When they fall back into the romantic ideal of the magic of the moon, their life is happiness and bliss. The moon teaches them about the magic they share. Eventually, they are able to live in a balanced love, combining physical love and spiritual love.

Nick's physical connection spurs her to contemplate higher matters as an ideal soul lover should. In spite of his effect, Susy attempts to keep the business element of their relationship at the forefront. Yet, the longer they remain under the influence of the moon, the more Susy becomes aware of their connection to nature and to each other. Eventually "she was aware only of the warm current running from palm to palm, as the moonlight below them drew its line of magic from shore to shore" (4). As their guiding light, the moon's magic and romance connecting the two shores also connects Nick's and Susy's body and spirit. They feel that the moon pulls them "outside of time and space," enabling them to be "one flesh" looking at the water (4–5). They are one, united in body and soul, and feel bliss in a way that no other character in Wharton's novels have up to this point.

Eventually, it is the belief that their love is a business arrangement that corrupts their happiness. As Susy contemplates the time they shall part, Nick reads the signs of nature as pointing to them to the realities of married life (5). Nick, at this point in their relationship, is more of an idealist than Susy. He is free to think of settling down because he feels that at Como they are beyond cares (4). The real world does not intrude into his fantasy of romance and marriage. Still, he does not share his views with Susy, because a permanent tie is not part of their venture. Their business agreement is what keeps them from a perfectly complete union even though all signs point to a different path for them. When they are together, they are blissfully happy and secure in each other (6). When they are together at Como, nothing else matters. Eventually, Susy begins to think that he "not only understood her, but" had similar ideas (5). They are acting like soul mates in the Republic, even though they subconsciously wish to deny their deeper union. Although Susy had always known there was a strong friendship between them both, they never would have discovered their true connection if they had not attempted this marriage venture.

Although they appear to build their marriage upon an unfeeling business transaction, it really is built upon much more. They are equals, comrades, partners in the venture. Their magic is that they form a whole with nature and with each other. Even Nick felt "it was worth all the past might have cost, and every penalty the future might exact of him" as long as they were together, alone in their shared bliss (20). For one month, they were able to live the dream that Wharton denied to so many of her earlier characters. This dream will not last long; for at the close of the month, they are forced to leave the place where they are whole. Susy corrupts the leaving the Republic by taking Strefford's cigars to accommodate Nick's physical needs. Although Susy did steal the cigars, she thought it was acceptable since she was doing it to make Nick's life better, not for her own gain (29). Her actions were to make another person happy, and thus, in her mind, justified. Her focus is still on the earthly, material needs, so she does not realize that she can provide him with such pleasure by fulfilling their spiritual bond. Instead, she believes that she needs to demonstrate her love through physical acts of love. This small slip into the realm of earthly desires begins Susy's fall from grace. Every mistake she makes from this point onward becomes a small sacrifice of her being to make Nick happy, safe and secure. However, her making these mistakes seems justified, considering that the understanding of their relationship is to provide for each other's needs.

The most detrimental blow to their happiness is Susy sacrificing her morality by becoming an accomplice in Ellie's affair. Ostentatiously done so that Nick can write his masterpiece, the act corrupts Susy not only in the physical realm, but also in the spiritual realm. For Nick, this sacrifice is the ultimate betrayal. It implies that Susy takes the marriage pact lightly and that she was not a pure, innocent woman. Once this sort of corruption takes place, Susy begins to rely on her cosmetics which enhance the "pale and haggard" look that appears on her face when she begins to lie to Nick (33). Her physical beauty begins to deteriorate once her spirit has been corrupted. Susy enhances this look so she can avoid Nick in order to protect his soul from the taint she feels. The avoidance and the lies make them no longer equals able to love each other.

Despite the lies and secrets, Nick and Susy still feel some elements of happiness. He is able to spend his time writing while she becomes a maternal figure for Clarissa Vanderlyn. Although they are the only two adults in the house, they spend more time apart than together. Nick spends most of his time writing and Susy spends her time caring for Ellie's daughter. In spite of this separation, her sacrifice almost seems worth the price at this point. Nick is being productive. Clarissa needs a maternal figure in her life while Ellie was gone. Without Susy's agreeing to Ellie's terms, Nick never would have been able to write and the servants would have ignored the child (41). The "philosophic romance" he writes, however, not only defines his novel, but also his treatment of Susy (41). He becomes increasingly involved in his dream of a romance of the soul at the expense of spending time with Susy in the earthly, physical realm. In creating this sort of romance, he also idealizes Susy beyond her abilities.

The first two sets of intruders into their world, Strefford and the Hickses, are also the people to whom Nick and Susy will run when they separate. Neither Strefford, nor Coral have the imagination to keep Susy or Nick. While Strefford has a "little imagination" (205), Coral knows she has not "enough imagination" but must "push" her way through life (236). Their first visitor, Strefford, who is comfortable in society and other realms, is perhaps the most able to understand Nick and Susy's relationship (40). In spite of their closeness, however, he too is complicit in Ellie and Algie's affair, which eventually taints him in Susy's eyes. However, before she learns of his complicity in the affair, Susy enjoys his company when Nick is too busy for her. Strefford notices, much as Nick noticed with Nat and Grace, the beneficial effects of the marriage and their happiness upon the newlyweds (46).

While Susy moves farther and farther out of their Republic, Nick creates a fantasy world for them both. In this fantasy, Susy replaces Nick's dead mother by giving him someone to be responsible to once again (54). In doing this he connects Susy with the dead Lansing women throughout history. As he begins to think of her as his property, "she had taken her place in the long line of Lansing women who had been loved, honoured, and probably deceived by bygone Lansing men" (54). He is, at this point, trying to write her history for her, placing her in a passive role and himself in the active role of the deceiver. What Nick does not realize is that Susy is deceiving him. The very act of deception which ruins their time together is also an assertion of Susy's living her own life and writing her own story. Not only is it an act against him, making him a passive, dead being, but it also equates Susy with sex and life.

Once the other members of their set begin crashing in upon their idyll, their lives begin to fall apart. Nick reaches a difficult point in his book, so he stops writing. He becomes disappointed not only because he must acknowledge that his friends create disenchantment in him but also because Susy is more alive when their friends are around. In essence, it is just another way for her to reject the story he is trying to create for her. He is disappointed that she does not feel the same way he does, but he does not talk to her about it either. For Nick, their friends are the same as always, but his uninterrupted time with Susy in the Republic awakened him to a more meaningful friendship (57). Yet, he believes she is not fully aware of what is going on in his mind. He believes she only "instinctively adopts" his views and begins to wonder if the "duet" of their lives will be his "solo" (57). He feels this way because they are no longer equal partners; he desires more from her than just a business venture. Nick, as it turns out, has relinquished all thoughts of the business foundation of their marriage (58). Susy's actions around their guests, however, lead him to believe that she does not feel the same way.

Jealousy creeps into Nick's paradise when Fred Gillow arrives. Fred, however, gives no sign of wanting to be anything other than to be on the outskirts of their party (61). As their private paradise becomes more and more distant for Nick and Susy, their lunar guide disappears from the story. They trade their moonlight meetings for sunset sails on the lagoon as they become more and more entrenched in the earthly realm. Susy must sacrifice herself to Strefford and Ellie to maintain Nick's ignorance of the world and keep him in his blissful paradise as much as possible. Her ultimate sacrifice is to keep his illusion that she had never known any other life than the one he desires for her. Eventually, Nick forces her to pretend she had an ignorance of physical love that her married friends had told her about long ago (70–71). Nick's ability to maintain the illusion of Susy's innocence is more shocking to their friends than the actual fact of Susy's knowledge.

In a not-so-subtle backgrounding to Susy's capers, the music surrounding them predicts her situation. As she tells Strefford of her role in Ellie's affair, a composer sings, "What of soul was left, I wonder" (71). The answer regarding Susy at this point is not much. She has, in effect, temporarily and unwittingly lost her soul. This leaves nothing for Nick and Susy's ideal love to live upon. In fact, it completely distances them and makes her a hallowed-out shell, essentially dead and soulless. After she has made her pact with Strefford, Nick notices a physical change in her. He finds that "to her old lightness of line was added a shadowy bloom, a sort of star-reflecting depth. Her movements were slower, less angular; her mouth had a nestling droop" (80). In essence, she looks as if she is suffering, carrying the weight of the world upon her shoulders, and slowly dying.

Nick's view of the situation is much different. Angry at Ellie's husband for his blindness, yet blind himself to Susy's actions, Nick continues to write a fiction of their life together. He hopes to be able to support Susy with his fiction writing and dreams of their living "in the attic of some tumble-down palace, above a jade-green waterway with a terrace overhanging a scrap of neglected garden" (76). Interestingly enough, Nick has these visions during "the Venetian summer" (76). The scent of dead fruits just enables him to write his dream of their ideal life. This ideal world of his, however, has elements of a faux Republic. Their neglected garden, surrounded by green water is not the airy heights of a true Republic.

As Susy comes to believe that she has changed, her world comes crashing down around her. During their argument over her role in Ellie's affair, Susy thinks "that nothing mattered except their love for each other" and that she could rescue them from greater harm "if only she could be sure of reaching a responsive chord in him" (87). Yet, that "responsive chord" is not struck and Nick's faith in her is gone. He flees offended by her complicity in Ellie's affair and disenchanted with Susy's love. Although he acknowledges that their parting will hurt and that their compact should never have been taken seriously, he cannot allow himself to be with her (91).

After they part, Nick spends his time trying to numb himself to the pain. He uses coffee to keep himself semi-conscious (Killoran 78). He even admits that he had actively sought out the passive life he finds with the Hickses (102). During this passivity he confronts the notion of unrequited love in the form of Mr. Buttles. Before leaving, Mr. Buttles attempts to gain one last look at his love, Coral. Mr. Buttles, it seems, would be happy just to live in the presence of his love. He believes, however, that she has fallen for another man (204). This, juxtaposed with Nick's parting glance of Susy and his quick judgment of her, places Nick as the negative, unfaithful love and of casting spells to separate lovers. Instead of seeking the last glance of a lover, he misreads the vision he sees of Susy. He has lost his faith in her and their love. He feels that Susy's soul is barren. Thinking that she had fallen back to her old ways, he crushes her fallen rose on the floor of the gondola (108). Smashing the rose is, in effect, his attempt to smash his love for her and wipe her out of his life. For a while, it works.

He no longer pictures an acceptable future for him and Susy. In fact, he can only think of Susy in a world he cannot, and will not, provide for her due to the social compromises which that form of life requires (109). There is no option for a future for them so he decides to set her free. Although he vows he will never remarry, he quickly and instinctively falls back into his old habit with the Hickses. He retreats from life to "visions of fleeing landscapes...and visions of study" (147). These visions were to keep him from the pain and the memories. In a way, it is like a drug-induced, death-like coma. He isolates himself from society, dead to his friends, dead to action and dead to daily cares. This death-in-life is Nick's only way of dealing with the loss of his soul mate.

In another act of creating a fantasy world, he begins to see the Hickses as saving him (149). Part of this salvation comes from his being able "to get away from sentiment, from seduction, from the moods and impulses and flashing contradictions that were Susy" (151). He runs from everything that is Susy and that reminds him of her. More importantly, he runs to the woman he believes is her complete opposite, Coral, who he believes is more concerned to intellectual pursuits (151). Whereas Susy is beautiful, Coral is "almost handsome" (152). Whereas Susy is sentiment, Coral is fact. Yet, whereas Susy is Nick's soul mate, Coral is just a shadow of what love could be. She will never have the ability to reach his deeper feelings, no matter how hard she tries (153). There will never be the communion of body and soul for Nick and Coral. He honestly believes he could settle for the kind of happiness Coral can provide (254), even though she cannot touch his soul as Susy has (255). Susy taught him the "belief in the immortality of loving," but life with Coral provides him the ability to live in oblivion (259). This sort of life is only acceptable to him as long as they can stay away from the rest of the world.

When society intrudes on Nick's life with the Hickses, forcing him to contemplate life again, he feels that the Hickses have become corrupted. Coral's impending engagement to the Prince makes Nick realize that until he married Susy, he had no connection with the future (198). Yet, to make that future come true, he must relinquish some of his idealized views of her. That is too difficult for Nick to release at this point. He believes that although he cannot live her life "that loving her roused in him ideals she could never satisfy" (232). In essence, he is awakened to the paradox of his love. In loving her, he idealized her, which set her up for the ultimate failure and pain. Yet, he still desired her body and soul. In essence, he wanted the complete love which so few people had ever felt (232–233). He wants a balance of body and soul in loving her.

Once they have separated, Susy's life is an awakening to pain, suffering and disillusionment. Their separation also brings about an increase in death imagery. While she is joking about Nick marrying Coral, her face turns exceedingly pale. When she sees herself in a mirror, she responds that the mirror makes her look "fished up from the canal" (95). She knows she looks deathly, but does not wish to attribute it to the loss of her soul mate. This is the reverse of what Charity saw in the mirror when she first finds a man who appeals to her physical desire. Susy, however, blames the looking-glass, not wanting to admit that the change has really taken place in her. Like George Darrow in *The Reef*, her past is written on her face. It is the loss of her love, her soul mate, and the fear that he has found her replacement, coupled with his lack of faith in her, which turns her into a corpse. As they plan on crashing the Hickses party, Strefford points out that her face continues to be a deathly image of what it formerly was (97).

Although Susy thinks Nick's return will restore their life together to its ideal state, he remains absent. The longer he stays away, the more her life lacks significance (99). She has lost everything that was dear to her. Being left alone in the physical realm is not what she had pictured for her life. She shrinks from the light of day (99). She wishes for a suffocating death. In essence, by blocking out the light she blocks out life and turns her room into a coffin. She does not want to face a world where her soul mate has lost all his faith in her and in their love. This is not the world she wants after the love she had experienced with Nick earlier.

When she awakens from her coffin-like, darkened room, it is to perform "some funeral rite" in burning Nick's letter and entering the new world in which she must live (100). This world is truly new to her. She begins to see her friends as he sees them. Instead of rejoining the friends who had always amused her in the past, she desires to retreat into isolation to take stock of her life (118). Her friends no longer hold the appeal they had in the past and she still feels alone. The moon, previously linked to her life with Nick, is no longer their guiding force; they have lost their magical love. Instead, Susy becomes linked with the rain. It is at this point, when she is broken-hearted over their separation, that the rain begins (117). It appears again when she receives the letter from Nick asking for a divorce (250), when Nick sees Strefford meeting her at night (259), and when Susy thinks that she has lost Nick forever (279). In essence, the rain appears when Susy believes that Nick has lost faith in her love. The rain will appear one final time, at the end of the novel. That rain, however, is just "a few drops" which are squelched by the moon (297).

While Susy is coming to terms with the full impact of the loss of her soul mate's faith, she is privy to a display of complete faith in love when she reunites with Nat and Grace. Although Nat is gaining in popularity with the social set, he still belongs to Grace, his soul mate (120). In many ways, the Fulmers' relationship parallels Nick and Susy's. Yet, as Nick and Susy become popular with their set, their relationship falls apart instead of becoming stronger. As Nat and Grace become popular, their relationship takes a few hits, but they remain equals and stay together. Their shared love, faith and memories are what will keep them together, no matter who tries to interfere with their relationship. Any interference, as Grace tells Susy, does not matter to her "in the balance…of one's memories" (143). The memories are the bond keeping them together in spite of outside forces.

Susy's time at Violet's house continues to open her eyes. She becomes aware that a person can be alone while surrounded by people and elects to remove herself from society to spend her time with her memories (124). Yet, her memories are of everything she had lost when Nick left. She realizes that her actions and the loss of his love have caused her to fall from a better world, the world she had experienced with Nick. With that world shut to her, she begins to wonder if the earthly world was where she should stay "since the other, the brief Paradise of her dreams" was no longer available (128–129). It appears that she is able to realize how fallen she is from this dreamlike idyll only after she has left it. When they were together, she focused more on the physical, material well-being and taking their spiritual connection for granted. With paradise shut, she needs to find a second option for her life.

That second option becomes apparent when the death of Strefford's relative elevates him to the most eligible man that she knows, a Lord. Now he can provide her with a better opportunity, the kind that Nick and Susy were discussing when entering their business marriage. His new status allows him to provide her with what she thought she wanted before her marriage, significant money and companionship. She had always seen him as being different from the rest of their friends, being able to mock them, and had always enjoyed his company, yet his poverty was a hindrance. Now that his status had been elevated, he would appear to be her ideal mate. Yet, ultimately, she rejects him because she has known something rarer, better with Nick.

Circumstances conspire against Susy. She visits Grace, her image of a one pure and faithful love, but finds her changed as a result of Nat's success. A hungry materialism that Susy finds abhorrent replaces Grace's old way of living. Shortly after this visit, Susy comes to the realization that her friends did not have her best interest in mind, but were just using her (145). It is at this point, that Susy becomes aware of what she believes she would need to reclaim her soul. It is through wealth, according to Susy and the people around her, that she could own her soul (146). However, she has no wealth and, therefore, no way of reclaiming her soul. Her belief that wealth is the only way to get her soul back forces her to contemplate Strefford's marriage proposal. Yet, that conclusion is false. As Wharton has shown throughout, it is faith in one's love and one's soul mate which will allow one to reclaim one's soul. It is faith in loving an equal partner that will help her reclaim her soul. Susy has not learned this yet.

The thought of owning her soul makes Susy waiver. She was uncertain if she could return to Nick and their makeshift way of life (158). Her seeing a way of owning her soul makes her question the life of love they had once shared. She wondered why they felt they were entitled to the life they once had (159). The life of luxury was not meant for them. Instead, Nick could only promise Susy a life of fiction and fantasy. Yet, her future with Strefford does not look like unqualified happiness either. Although he would provide for all her physical needs, it could never be a real love of equal souls. Instead, her life with Nick was the reality she wanted to know (159). It was that life which "had given her besides the golden flush of her happiness, the sudden flowering of sensuous joy in heart and body" (159). There is, however, no sign of her being able to reclaim that life with him, since she believes he is off with Coral, creating a new life.

It takes a separation from Nick for her to appreciate what they had together. While they were a couple, she often overlooked "the deep disquieting sense of something that Nick and love had taught her, but that reached out even beyond love and beyond Nick" that was in their relationship (159). Once again the word beyond appears when discussing the ideal love of one soul for another. Susy finally realizes that the love they shared is beyond each of them and uniting them at the same time. There was a strength in their love that not only connected them to each other but to the world and the lovers beyond. They have become one with each other and the past. Nick taught her about love beyond the physical, earthly love. Instead, he touched her soul in ways no one else could. It is because she is aware of something greater, a love in the Republic, that she cannot return to her old ways and marry Strefford. The future he offers her, although materially satisfactory, will never touch her soul.

Although she toys with the idea that as Strefford's wife she would have the wealth to create an ideal world, she realizes she must create it alone (180). The world she would be creating with Strefford's money, however, would be a faux Republic. It would have all the physical trappings of a Republic, but Nick would not be by her side. Marriage to Strefford would perhaps provide the means to create the paradise, but not the like mind, the shared soul, or the imagination to enter it. In fact, when trying to communicate her feelings to Strefford, she recognized the limits of his imagination and understanding (228). Once she realizes this, everything about Strefford becomes inferior. His kiss is distasteful because they are not Nick's lips touching hers. She knows that there is a chance that Strefford's kiss will become less abhorrent, but it will never show her the world beyond that Nick's kiss did.

With the belief that Nick really and truly no longer wants her, "she felt herself dropping down into the bottomless anguish…but she was weary of anguish: her healthy body and nerves instinctively rejected it. The wave was spent, and she felt herself irresistibly struggling back" (200–201). She cannot and will not die because he left her, even though her soul may want to. Instead, the physical realm has a tight grasp on her and her youth struggles to survive. She may never find love with Nick again, but she will not die from his leaving her. Yet, the kind of life available to her is in question. Her attempts to throw herself into life with Strefford fail. He no longer is the entertaining companion of her past, but a dull, pompous, hearing impaired man (204). In a phrase, he is not Nick. The final straw for Susy occurs when she learns he rented his house to Ellie and Algie for their affair. This is the ultimate betrayal of her because not only was he an accomplice in the affair, but he also tainted her earthly paradise by allowing inferior beings to inhabit it. She can no longer go on with the charade of a potential marriage to Strefford. Although she believes that Nick will marry Coral, she would rather be alone than married to the man who corrupted their earthly paradise.

Once she arranges for her freedom, death again surrounds Susy. Society life becomes completely fake and unsatisfying (221). Aware of the results of her change, "she seemed to be looking at it all from the other side of the grave;...she felt as if the glittering avenue were really changed into the Fields of Shadows...and as if she were a ghost among ghosts" (221). She has reached the level of the dead woman, a ghostly shadow of her former self. She is finally ready for Nick to re-enter her life. When Nick does return to her, she becomes an idealized version of her former self. His seeing her as the ideal mother awakens him to her potential. Not only does he rediscover his love for her, he also continues to write the story of her life for her. This vision allows him to claim her as his own, as part of his soul. However, Strefford's appearance easily shatters his faith in their love. Susy's and Nick's first face-to-face meeting after their separation fails because neither is willing to declare their feelings for fear of causing complications for the other. Instead of being honest, Susy wishes him well with Coral and he asks about the Fulmers' divorce. Susy's conversation about the Fulmers having to be together because they are connected is a subtle hint to Nick (247). Although neither one wants to admit it, Nick and Susy have been "through such a lot together" that they belong to each other (247).

Only after he is gone does she realize how much she loves Nick. She understands that the "impulse" she felt for him at the beginning was love (277). She had not realized the extent of her feelings for him, though, until she had lost him and they had been through such pain in separating. She also knows that "this was something so much larger and deeper that the other feeling seemed the mere dancing of her blood in tune with his" (277). They have gone beyond the physical, earthly love and found a deeper spiritual connection that they cannot sever, no matter what they do. They have a shared bond even in their separation. Yet, she cannot believe that this sort of love could be unfulfilled so she must wonder if it were the average love that had scared her (277). The mere fact that they doubted each other prevented their making their love the ideal spiritual love, the romance of the soul.

Once they finally admit their true feelings to themselves, they run to reunite. They realize that marriage, for them, could only be with each other. For a brief moment, they are happy once again. They are even able to work out the intrusion of the Fulmer children on their paradise, yet Wharton once again is unable to leave her characters with a blissfully happy life. Susy's concern for their material well-being brings a shadow upon their new happiness, much as her taking the cigars did earlier. Nick, caught up in the idealized version of their relationship, does not see the need for the material well-being, but Susy does. She is, in effect, more practical about their love, even though she is also willing to acknowledge her full spiritual connection with him. She has changed, but she has not become his idealized woman. Instead, the novel ends with Nick and Susy in the same physical position as at the beginning, yet at a different place both emotionally and spiritually. Although she has made a mistake by believing in the satisfaction of physical needs, Nick realizes he is not as morally superior as he once was. He has not broken his engagement to Coral, the reason she did not marry the prince, yet he is running off with his wife instead of divorcing her. He is not as blameless as he would like to believe.

In the end, several elements return to welcome them back to their paradise, the rain, the moon and the "troubled glory" which promises to be their guiding influence throughout their married life together (297). Although they are happy and will be together, it will not be an unmarred, blissful happiness. Instead, Wharton leaves the reader with the "troubled glory" of Nick and Susy (297). The cycle of their love has come full circle, but with a new understanding between them. There is a physical and spiritual love that people can find, nurture, and believe in while alive, but there is not complete and total happiness in this Republic. The members are not pure and innocent, but they are not totally corrupt either. It is neither a truly deadly future, nor a truly glorious future. Their love is, finally, a love of equals, not a business partnership (224). Yet, as long as they have faith in their love and in each other, their love will survive and grow.

CHAPTER NINE
Twilight Sleep

Following on the heels of Nick and Susy's qualified happiness between less than perfect soul mates is what could be Wharton's most cynical view of love. *Twilight Sleep* presents several options regarding love, but no concrete solutions as to how to achieve love and happiness. Wharton presents a picture of failed spiritual relationships and failed physical relationships with no complete union of body and soul. Instead, this novel is about Nona's education into love along with revealing where Wharton's theory of love is at this point. Although Nona comes to learn that excessive soul love and excessive physical love can be harmful, there is no form of love left in which she can believe. She has, it appears, lost all faith in love by the end of her education.

Wharton depicts Nona's education into the ways of love through the romantic relationships that surround her throughout the novel. Her own relationship with Stanley Heuston is typical of the relationships Wharton presents in her early career; they believe their souls are connected, but they cannot move into a complete union because of an obstacle, in this case Heuston's wife. In the opening pages of the novel, Nona's love for Heuston is a spiritual love that will never become anything more than like minds due to his marriage to Aggie. Nona is an interesting creation in that she belongs "to the bewildered disenchanted young people" (12), but she also belongs to a past world which believed in an idealized love (46). Despite her belief that she is truly modern, Arthur Wyant fascinates her because she envisions him to be a "romantic figure" from an era of which she longs to be a part (42). Wyant, however, is an obsolete creature in the world about them, like a creature in a museum, as indicated by his nickname (13). He is no longer a part of the world, but an exhibit for the living to observe as a product of a bygone age. Given that Nona meets up with Heuston under the watchful eye of the "faded" romantic figure of Wyant, it should come as no surprise that her love for Heuston represents the romantic notion of a spiritual union of two souls (42). Her love also reveals itself through physical manifestations signified in sexual selection. The mention of his name evokes a passionate blush to her cheeks (40). Though her words for him express a different feeling towards Heuston, her blush reveals her true feelings. She is not, however, concerned with a physical union because "no one understood her as well as" he did (47). Although her brother is family, even he does not have the complete understanding of her that she believes Heuston has. His understanding her is a strong aphrodisiac for a girl fascinated with romantic notions. It allows her to believe in the romantic ideal of soul mates. Heuston's understanding signifies a belief in her and their love that is stronger than a family bond.

In many ways, Nona's and Heuston's love have elements in common with courtly love. For in courtly love, "the essence of...love was protracted excitement, a delirium of gorgeously unbearable longing" (Ackerman 54). Love becomes a game which elevated and idolized the woman and was "bound by the rules of...secrecy, patience, and moderation—the last was not altogether synonymous with chastity, but meaning rather restraint" (De Rougemont 76). Throughout the novel, their relationship follows De Rougemont's description. Although the "weekly meetings with him...[are] the one thing in her life that gave it meaning," she kept her feelings hidden as much as possible from her family (142). Even though they cannot be together in a completely acknowledged union, Nona lives for their few moments together. Even at moments when she questions their relationship, "every nerve in her told her that these moments were the best thing in life, the one thing she couldn't do without: just to be near him, to hear his cold voice, to say something to provoke his disenchanted laugh; or better still, to walk by him as now without talking . . ." (143). This bond is the foundation of a spiritual union in Wharton's works. As in her previous works, once Nona becomes conscious of the extent of their connection, a twinge of the deathly aura does emerge. At the height of her realizing how much she loves Heuston, she also comprehends that she can give a mortal end to her love and life whenever she desires (143). If she wishes, she could end their relationship on earth with her death, allowing greater idealization of her in Heuston's mind. Yet, despite her admiration of romantic ideals of love, she is partially modern so she cannot act upon those thoughts. She has progressed from the world of the dead Lily Bart and Bessy Westmore. She wants something more from life and her love for Heuston, who does appear to love her also.

Perhaps due to her romantic nature or a desire to keep her relationship with Heuston on a spiritual level, she refuses to share any physical relationship with him until he is single again. Since they both believe that Aggie will never divorce him, this refusal acts to keep their relationship on the spiritual level and prolong the focus on moderation of their love. Yet, Stanley's relationship with Aggie does not just serve as an impediment to their finding a fulfilling union; it also serves as a warning to Nona of the emptiness of a solely spiritual love. Aggie and Nona, in fact, are quite similar. Both love Heuston, both are fond of the past (200) and both are "saints" in their relationships with others (201). Nona sees a slight difference in her sainthood, however, in that she has a different style than Aggie (201). In spite of their similarities and Aggie's love for Heuston, Aggie only offers him an extreme form of a spiritual union that has evolved into a religious devotion for him and the church. Assuming that Aggie and Heuston did have a solely spiritual union, the foundation of their love seems very similar to Heuston's and Nona's love. Aggie, in fact, thought they had "always lived together on the most perfect terms . . ." (202). Living on those terms, however, is not enough to make their love a complete union. Nona sees a problem in the fact that Heuston and Aggie never argued. Their souls never experience any passion. Aggie does not quite understand, but turns to Nona to learn the secret passion Nona knows (203). In not having the passion of arguments and the fact that they did not have children, one can conclude their life together evolved into a passionless devotion. Nona, distanced from this relationship, is able to see it as Heuston and Aggie "be[ing] sacrificed to a sterile union—as sterile spiritually as physically—to miss youth and love" (179). Although Nona's interpretation is biased, she is accurate in seeing their union as a "sacrifice" evolving into an unfulfilling relationship for at least one member. Aggie has sacrificed her passion for a spiritual love.

Yet, in spite of this excessive spirituality, Aggie believes in her love for Heuston (181). It was just that her "love was…a sort of fleshless bony affair . . ." (181). Aggie feels her duty and love is not just to God, but to God through her husband. The thought of living for God in man also appears in *The Fruit of the Tree*, where Amherst wanted to have his wife live for God in him. For Amherst that is the ideal, but for Heuston it is the ultimate corruption and impediment to love. In depicting this, Wharton has come to the point in her theory of love where the complete spiritual union is not the most desired love between a man and a woman. In fact, spiritual love without a physical love is unfulfilling and as harmful as a purely physical love. The ultra-spiritual love that Aggie offers Heuston serves as a warning to Nona. It is because of this warning that Nona refuses to step into the role of Heuston's savior. Although upon first hearing Aggie's willingness to set her husband free, "Nona's mind, racing forward, touched the extreme limit of human bliss...then crawled back from it bowed and broken-winged" (204). The image recalls that of Justine's winged love drawn from Plato. Yet, Nona knows this is not the fulfilling love she could have. The thought of being with him is thrilling until Nona realizes Aggie is releasing him only if she will save him from the super-sexual, super-physical and super-modern Cleo Merrick. Nona, however, does not want to have to save him because she has also seen how detrimental that sort of love can be in observing Eleanor's and Wyant's love.

Wyant's and Eleanor's relationship receives the least amount of attention, but is another version of what Nona's and Heuston's love can evolve into if she takes on the role of his savior (26). Although, Pauline believes that Eleanor is the woman who broke up her marriage to Wyant that may not truly be the case. Whatever her role was in the dissolution of the marriage, Wyant became responsible for Eleanor, who becomes his caretaker for life at the expense of her life. She has no visitors or existence outside of Wyant and Jim's yearly visit. Yet, she does not seem bothered by her lack. She is the sacrifice for Wyant's love. To the family, she was the one whom "Wyant had never married...[but] had never deserted" (40). One even wonders if this would have been Zeena's fate if Ethan had not married her. She is invisible to the rest of the world, except in relation to Wyant. Eleanor has no real identity of her own and lives a life of shadows because she sacrificed herself to Wyant as Aggie asked Nona to sacrifice herself to Heuston. Nona realizes this would be her fate if she accepts Aggie's offer and refuses to sacrifice herself for such a love.

Given that the spiritual solution does not seem fully satisfying, Nona and Heuston attempt to move their love into the physical realm. It is only after the thoughts of death that this happens, even though she eventually realizes that if she kept meeting him, he would want more which may not be the best thing for everyone involved (143). She knows his dinner invitation is to give them time together (144) which will culminate in a kiss they had never previously shared. She rationalizes her agreeing to acquiesce to the date by thinking of it as

> a friendly evening, an evening of simple comradeship, that…could give her back her youth, yes and, the courage to persevere. She put her hand through his arm, and knew by his silence that he was thinking her thoughts. That was the final touch of magic. (144)

Despite the inadequacy of the fully spiritual union, Nona needs to believe that their friendship is the key to their being together. Throughout Wharton's works this camaraderie has always been reserved for soul mates. Nona and Stanley have a barrier they cannot overcome. Although Nona does know that there is more to the relationship than just the friendship, she is content to enjoy his company while he is near her. At the end of the evening, however, Heuston pushes for more than just a spiritual union. While she desires silence and perhaps avoidance of the physical love, he desires a kiss and a future. Heuston knows the emptiness of a purely, excessively, spiritual union, having lived through it with Aggie. He wants more and believes that Nona can satisfy his desire for both a physical and spiritual union. He thinks Nona is free enough to be able to provide him with something more. Interestingly enough, Heuston's way of forcing Aggie to divorce him is to turn to a woman who Aggie believes is physical passion personified.

If Aggie's love is to serve as a warning against extreme spiritual love, then Lita's relationships are an education in and warnings against extreme physical love. Despite Nona, Bee and Lita running in the same set, Nona is different from the other two due to her upbringing (57). Unlike Lita, she refuses to use her body to entice Klawhammer (79). Like Dexter, she believes it is her job to protect Lita and Lita's family from Lita's destructive physical love. Lita and Bee live a life of physical love, Lita so much so that Nona and others acknowledge that "Lita was to be worshipped" due to the fact that she always looked like a specimen of physical perfection (16–17). Everything about Lita suggests Darwinian physicality. She has the lazy luxury of a woman with a desirable body and who is fully aware of her desirability. People should worship her based on her physical beauty. It is her body and its movements which draw eyes to her in any setting. Her thoughts and morals are elements for which she has no time and in which others find her lacking. Her physical nature, however, captivates beyond words. Lita, however, is not ignorant of her body and how to display it. She paints her boudoir black in order to set of the beauty of her golden hair and her look of being "spun of spray and sunlight" (35). Her physical appearance will lighten even the darkest room. Even Klawhammer wants to hire her based on just a still picture of her body in movement.

Lita's purely physical love serves to warn Nona against extreme physical passion. Initially, Nona believes that Lita's relationship with Jim was good not only because they were in love, but also because they were able to produce offspring. They have fulfilled the rules of sexual selection and they have passed the best traits on to the next generation. Nona, however, is mistaken. Although their marriage was not destructive, Lita is constantly seeking someone else and Jim is forced to settle down into a job he despises in order to provide for their physical needs (30). He works too much and is absent from the family he loves in order to care for Lita's physicality. This change in his lifestyle elicits an equivalent change in his looks. He had lost "all the wild uncertain things" that others loved in him and all that "was left now was all the plain utility" (35). He is not living a life of love and excitement, but has become another toy for Lita to use in satisfying her physical needs. She becomes restless because there is no completeness in just a physical love. As a result of this unfulfilling side of their life, the baby, the one positive sign of their good, physical love and its nursery are neglected (191). Things are not as they should be in the baby's room from the "soiled towels" to the "dead and decaying flowers" (192). This neglect shows that she is a negligent mother in not caring for her child and forcing him to fend for himself. She lacks the instincts to nurture her young so that she can concentrate on pursuing another mate. In a way, she takes on the role that Darwin assigns to men in order to produce "the largest number of offspring" (2:403). In fact, the only time she spends with her child is when Dexter forces her to do so. Her neglect does not just manifest itself in the rearing of her offspring, but continues through all aspects of her marriage. However, no one can save the marriage unless and until she begins to see things differently.

As if this detrimental physical relationship and Lita's mesmerizing Klawhammer were not enough of a warning, Lita gets involved in a second physical relationship with Dexter. Although it is this relationship which preoccupies Nona throughout the majority of the novel, it is not the fact that Dexter has a fascination for another woman that is problematic, but the fact that the object of his infatuation is Jim's wife. The awkward aspect of the relationship for Nona is not the implications of incest, but the fact that Lita may hurt Jim with her actions. Since Dexter has a reputation for having a roving eye, Nona does not believe he will form a permanent attachment with Lita. Initially, Pauline and Nona both believe that he was infatuated with Gladys Toy (64) and Dexter actually kisses her before kissing Lita (231). Yet, this affair is not bothersome because it was "a perfectly normal elderly man's flirtation with a stupid woman he would forget as soon as he got back to town" (239). It was also an affair with a woman who was not concerned with only physical pleasures and knew her role. She is just a toy for Dexter's amusement. She would provide him with a bit of a diversion, perhaps a kiss or two, but nothing more serious or detrimental than that.

Lita, however, is different. Not only does she not know her place, but she also offers more than just an innocent flirtation. After all she admired, and perhaps even married, Jim because she thought he was Pauline's and Dexter's love child. As soon as she learns he was not the product of their illicit physical love she becomes even more disenchanted with him (196–197). She has created an image of Dexter's physical love consuming him so much so that he is willing to cross the boundaries that are normally assumed to be upheld. Yet, she soon learns that is not the case. Jim was not a love child and Dexter is slow to act upon his passion. Interestingly, Dexter's fascination with Lita concerns Nona the most when he has not fully formulated the idea of it or acted upon his feelings. Dexter, although he does acknowledge Lita's beauty, is initially more concerned with watching her to help save Jim's marriage (81). He does not entertain any romantic thoughts of her until later and, in fact, even dislikes her when she first enters the family. While tending to her, he conceives of an ideal version of Lita, which he tries to force upon her. She shatters that image, however, by placing the picture of her dancing in the paper for the world to see. The picture shows that she not only knows of the power of her physical love, but also openly acknowledges it. In fact, seeing the photo of Lita saved him from "sentiment" with her (163).

On some level, he does know that she is only concerned with physical love. He only started to like her as a member of the family once she gave birth to Jim's son, thus entering into the roles of mother and sexually experienced woman. However, "the enchantment did not last; he never recaptured it" (106). She never again became the beautiful Madonna with child. Instead, he cannot stand the thought of "what she was" (111). Once he realized that the birth did not add a depth of character to her that matched the "new shadowiness under her golden lashes," she no longer totally fascinates him (106). The death-like knowledge of physical love does not permeate her being. She remains a superficial entity who, at the most, is able only to arouse "a sort of irritated interest" in him (106). She is capable of no deeper feelings or thoughts even with her experience. Instead, Lita's mind is unskilled (14). She cannot see beyond her physical desires which only allows her to see half of the love she could have in life.

It is only after Lita shocks him out of his earlier idealized notion of her and Lita's jealousy toward Gladys that Dexter decides to truly embark on a physical relationship with her (256). Only the romantic figure, Wyant, comes to the rescue to put a stop to this relationship once and for all. Just as Aggie was a warning against disproportionate spiritual love, so Lita is a warning against disproportionate physical love. At this stage, Nona remains with no model relationship to follow. She has two divergent notions of love in which to believe, yet neither provides a sufficient way of completely living and loving another.

This lack of a model brings us to Pauline Wyant Manford. She has been the focus of the majority of scholarly discussions regarding *Twilight Sleep* and is often seen as Wharton's depiction of a person relentlessly seeking to avoid pain and unpleasantness. However, everyone in her family admires her (12). Pauline is, in fact, the ultimate warning for who Nona may become if she cannot find a balance between spiritual and physical love. Pauline has been through the search for the ideal romantic relationship in marrying Wyant and the ideal physical relationship in marrying Dexter. Since she too could not find a balance in love, she "uses science as religion" (Killoran 117). In marrying Wyant, she married the romantic ideal; in marrying Dexter, she married the physical ideal. However, she no longer receives the physical love that Dexter once provided. In fact, Pauline's illusions have come and gone regarding Dexter, and they have stopped being intimate (236). As the novel begins, she sees Wyant as a "failure" and it seems as if Dexter is heading in that direction also (25). For Pauline, the answer is no longer finding a balance in love, but searching elsewhere and everywhere for the balanced union she desires. Her search for feeling completely fulfilled begins with the physical healing of the Mahatma.

The Mahatma's concern is purely the body because "he was always celebrating the nobility of the human body" (96). He teaches Pauline about "holy ecstasy" through "physical culture" (29). He initially pulls her in with the promise that she is psychic, thus excessively spiritual (27), but then turns his attention to her body through eurhythmic exercises. The spiritual opening quickly devolves into physical, bodily pleasures as the exercises focus solely on physical fixes to problems. Yet, the purely physical approach is not a cure-all for Pauline's concerns. In fact, it becomes a huge scandal once Lita and Bee's picture is published in the paper.

With the corruption of the physical cure, she must find a new cure or be cut adrift without something in which to have faith. Once again, the initial appeal to begin the treatment is to proclaim Pauline to be psychic (120). This time, she finds a new healer, Alva Loft who "acts on you—on your spirit" to cure concerns (119). For a while, the cure appears to work. Yet, this cure is not the answer either. Pauline "had come to depend on it [the séance cure] as 'addicts' do on their" drugs (153). The treatment turns her into the equivalent of a drug fiend, never satisfied until she gets her next hit. Another drawback is that this treatment focuses solely on her spiritual side to the negation of the body, just as the Mahatma focused on the body to the exclusion of the spirit earlier. When events in Pauline's life reach a stress-level that Alva Loft cannot cure, she finds yet another savior.

Pauline trades in Loft's "mind which speaks to the *mind*" for Gobine's "immediacy: direct contact with the Soul of the Invisible" (273). Her new role model will take Pauline "out of the senseless rush and…Beyond the Veil" (273). Being brought "Beyond the Veil" reminds one of Selden's Republic of the Spirit and Lily Bart's calling card. Once again, we see the term "beyond" linked to a connection with a soul (273). She learns how to go beyond real world problems and cares. The novel ends before she is able to judge the full success of Gobine's treatment. Yet, if her reaction to Nona's shooting and later events are a sign, this treatment may actually work. Before Pauline leaves on her trip with Dexter, Nona also comes to wonder about the new treatments. She contemplates if they can provide her a "spiritual escape," just as the gunshot that wounded her provided her with a physical escape from the problems around her (306). In fact, Pauline's ability to rebound from the horror of the shooting surprises even Nona. Pauline does feel pain for her daughter at the time of the shooting, but the new treatments have taught her how to deal with it. Although Pauline is wearing make-up, she looks younger and as if she does not have a trouble bothering her (307). She has been born again to a new world and world which balances the body and the soul. She has finally awakened from her twilight sleep through the "sacrificial" shooting of her daughter (Wershoven 134).

Nona's education into the ways of love and death ends with her being shot in Lita's bedroom, the site of the start of Dexter's and Lita's physical affair. Her being clipped by Wyant's bullet in his attempt to stop the tryst saves her as much as it wounds her. The romantic bullet saves her from falling into the depression she is entering into before Wyant shoots her. Although her life is not in any grave danger from the wound, he shoots her at a time when she is in danger of losing herself and missing the lesson of love that all those around her are inadvertently teaching.

Instead, it is "Nona's blood spattering the silvery folds of the rest-gown" which shatters the twilight sleep of the others along with ruining the sleeping-gown (299). The wound forces Nona and her family out of their twilight sleep and into a new conception of love based on balance. The sacrifice of Nona's blood saves them all. Yet, they cannot deal fully with their awakening as seen in their leaving her. As Wershoven argues, "their flight from Nona, represents their awareness that Nona is not like them, that she will not join them in the search for easy answers and instant solutions" (135). While the rest of the family members are able to flee the scene of the crime, Nona stays to confront the situation and what she has learned. She knows that her story is false, yet no one wants to ask anything more from her (304). Wyant and Eleanor flee to Canada, Jim and Lita to Paris, and Pauline and Dexter travel around the world to allow her time to think. In spite of everyone leaving, Nona "was not sure that she wanted to go away at all—at least in the body. Spiritual escape was what she craved" (306).

Getting away from her thoughts and feelings, away from the pain of her winged soul, is no longer available to her since she has awakened from the twilight sleep of love. In order to dull the soul, she contemplates a return to the place where she was shot, the scene of the primacy of the body. She still has to learn how to make a successful relationship, but there is still no role model for her to follow. Nona has learned the emptiness of an excessive spiritual union and the pain and destructiveness of an excessive physical union, but has nothing to replace them. It is only after Pauline expresses her horror at Nona even suggesting what she thinks is an "old-fashioned" religious answer, does Nona add the caveat that the convent must be one "where nobody believes in anything" (315). In a way, this caveat is more for Pauline's happiness than Nona's. Nona does not believe in the faith of love. Instead, Nona is still searching for answers. By the end of the novel, the only conclusion she can reach is that it is best not to think about love in the modern world. It is only in Wharton's final work, *The Buccaneers*, that she is able to conceive of a truly happy, balanced union of body and soul for the characters.

CHAPTER TEN
The Buccaneers

The Buccaneers is Wharton's final statement on her theory of love and death in romantic relationships. Left unfinished at the time of her death, it is the work which finally explains all her earlier beliefs regarding relationships while allowing her central character to obtain the ultimate passionate union of physical and spiritual love. Interestingly, this ultimate union is based upon an understanding "about the *beyondness* of things," between soul mates (257). It was not until this final novel that Wharton had come completely to terms with the concept of balancing the love of the soul and the reality of physical love on earth.

In writing the stories of this group of young women entering society, Wharton depicts characters in what could be considered her most positive, and perhaps happiest, portrayal of romantic relationships (Wershoven 162). With the exception of Mabel Elmsworth, each girl embarks on a relationship based on a different physical, emotional or spiritual foundation. Perhaps Mabel's exclusion is due to the fact that Wharton left the novel unfinished, or perhaps it was because she was only created to assist in her sister's relationship. In any case, the other four girls make socially successful matches. It is through the character of Annabel St. George, who had no vocabulary to speak of "the events or emotions below the surface of life," that Wharton is finally able to reveal her concept of an idealized union encompassing both spiritual and physical love, to depict a relationship beyond the two people involved, allowing them to find a balanced love (422–423).

Although Wharton reserved the ultimate union for Nan and Guy, the other relationships formed by the girls assist in explaining her view of love. We learn the least about the relationship between the most beautiful girl, Virginia St. George, and the most eligible bachelor, Lord Seadown

Brightlingsea. Most of what Wharton depicts of their relationship is a courtship based on shared pity for each other. In this way, they become equals in feeling. When Jinny first meets Seadown, she does not comment on his beauty, or money, or any element of sexual selection which would make him a promising match. Instead, she says that she "thought he looked pretty sad, too; like all the others" in his family (250). Her attraction to him is that he stirs in her a kindred emotion of sympathy and a desire to help him realize happiness. Most likely, although not overtly mentioned, his impending title and wealth do attract Virginia, but it is the fact that she feels sympathy for Seadown that first appeals to her (253). The other girls are not blind to the fact that Seadown needs a woman to show him sympathy in order to win his heart. As Conchita points out, all he needs is for a woman to relate to him on an emotional level to win his heart (251). For Virginia, it is his needing a sympathetic heart and mind that is most attractive.

Seadown's main desire for the girls is built upon sympathy also. He is torn between Jinny and Lizzy until he is able to feel pity for one of them (313). In fact, until pushed by sympathetic feelings, he is content to "lay at their feet, plucking…clover" since, as Robinson puts it, Seadown needed both girls to ignite his imagination (313). It is the embarrassment caused by Lady Churt's arrival and pity for Jinny which finally forces him into action. While the men stand back to observe Lady Churt's attack, which caused Virginia to stand in defiance of Lady Churt, it is Lizzy who comes to the immediate rescue (313). In the atmosphere of game-playing, Lizzy's asserting Virginia's claim to Seadown causes a stalemate between the women until Seadown acts to choose one of them. He does not act, however, until he sees Virginia's terrified tears. He had found her beautiful before, but it is not until he was able to empathize with her that he was willing to act and select her as a mate. Interestingly, Wharton leaves the reader speculating if they will go through with the marriage until the Duchess of Tintagel reads the announcement in the paper. From this point on, Virginia's marriage and life fade from the story. The narrative eventually mentions in passing that Jinny learns her peerage and that money is tight for them, but no more of their story is told. By building their marriage upon mutual pity, the two have a sympathetic and empathetic bond. Although theirs may not be the ideal marriage, it could be that their relationship is relatively happy. They entered into the marriage bond as equals in feeling and emotion.

Lizzy Elmsworth's love for Hector Robinson is another relationship which, although significant, has gaps in its story. Wharton bases the marriage on a mutual sentiment, which is neither physical love nor spiritual love. Although equal in beauty to Virginia, but with the added element of style, Robinson does not have strong feelings for Lizzy until she sacrifices her chances with Seadown to save Virginia (128). Prior to her sacrifice, he was content to watch her and her friends without any intention of marrying. Interestingly, after Robinson discovers his strong admiration for Lizzy, their relationship fades from the story until the end of the novel. Both characters have a strong ambitious drive in common. Hector wanted to increase in status as much as she did (308). He is ambitious. He has aspirations of joining the right social set. Lizzy is equally ambitious. She is jealous when she learns that Virginia and Nan are attending the last major event of the season, the Queen's drawing-room party (263). Lizzy, however, is smart enough not to let her jealousy interfere with her ambition and immediately begins plotting how she can use the St. Georges' good luck to her own benefit. She saw that they could help each other in conquering London society (271). Her ambition is the guiding force in her life and in creating a united front with her rivals for London's eligible bachelors.

It is this shared ambition, not any form of love previously seen in Wharton's works, upon which Lizzy and Hector build their marriage. In many respects, it does turn out to be a good marriage. Hector still believes that she is beautiful (471). He has possession of his father's lands and has reached the ambitions he had when he met Lizzy. In essence his dreams have been fulfilled (471). The two even have a baby to finish out the notion of the happy family and a productive union. Hector's and Lizzy's crowning achievement comes about when Lizzy tells him that the Duchess of Tintagel is coming to visit. Her visit, even though it is without the Duke, is a great honor and a sign of their having achieved an acceptable social status.

Hector's and Lizzy's matching social ambitions make it seem like they are a perfect match of equals. He sounds relatively content to have reached the heights he has by the final chapter we have of the novel. Underneath his contentment, however, Hector worries that she may leave him for higher social aspirations (473). He is afraid that her ambition will carry her beyond what he can provide her. Although he is content with the level they have reached and is ready to settle down to their happy union, Lizzy's ambitions, it seems, could be pushing her further. If this were to happen, the foundation of their life together would crumble. Only the thought of their baby upstairs, supposedly a sign of their bountiful union and not just an heir to the family fortune, puts his fears to rest. Yet, there will be forever this seed of doubt and worry for Hector. The remaining plot summary does not address whether or not Lizzy will make his fears come true.

Outside of Nan's two potential loves, the young girl whose relationships we know the most about is Conchita Closson's marriage and subsequent affairs. Conchita's youth is one in which romantic liaisons are encouraged and arranged by governesses (136). Although Nan is physically ill at the thought of a world where the governess assists and participates in these liaisons, she feels drawn to Conchita. They become friends and Nan thinks the world of her. Nan is also the first to tell Laura of Lord Richard's interest in Conchita, as if to have her governess assist in the liaison. Richard is not the best selection for her friend, however. Despite the rumors of his falling out with his family and the rush to wed (185), Conchita's mother insists in believing that her daughter's match was a good one, "a love-match" (191). There is some doubt in her mind, however. She needs Laura's reassurance that Richard really is "passionately in love with" her daughter (191). Interestingly, it could be in this early stage that he truly is passionately in love with her, along with her assumed monetary worth. If this match is one based on physical love, then the later events in their love calls into question the essential goodness of predominantly physical love matches.

Two years after their marriage, Conchita and Richard are in debt and both claim they were deceived in their match. For Richard, the deception concerns the amount of money her family has and for Conchita the deception is in the depth of Richard's physical love for her. Theirs is neither a marriage nor a love based on spiritual or emotional bonds, but a passionate physical and monetary promise. They do not talk to each other since physical passion was all they had in common (243). There appears to be no way to bring them to a spiritual or emotional connection. Yet, their marriage is successful according to sexual selection because they have a child.

Although Richard ventures into various trysts, Conchita's unhappiness reveals itself in physical manifestations. Her eyes "darken" as she speaks his name (243). Her pain and sadness, just like their love, has a physical manifestation. From this point forward, Conchita forms a series of physical matches with handsome men lacking the appropriate income (251). These relationships, however, are rarely more than passing mentions made over lists of party guests. They are not serious loves in her life, but they do provide her with temporary physical distractions that are lacking in her relationship with Richard. Yet, in spite of her disillusionment with Richard, she will not divorce him. She feels that living in London is worth paying the price of disillusionment.

Interestingly, when Conchita requests money from Nan, her approach is a romantic appeal. She says that not only is she completely in debt, but she is also "in love with one man while…tied to another" (419–420). She needs Nan's assistance because she "can't live without affection" and with her husband not providing it in her life, she must seek it elsewhere (422). While Nan envisions a way out, either through divorce or returning to New York, Conchita would rather stay married in England than return to a world which would be the death of her socially. Conchita's romantic predicament is problematic according to Nan (421). However, she does not think that it is the absolutely worst thing that could happen. In contemplating the situation, she questions if it might be better "with such a sin on one's conscience than in the blameless isolation of an uninhabited heart?" (421). The barrenness and loneliness that she feels at this point is worse than taking a lover. She is, in her own way, jealous of Conchita's ability to find physical passionate loves, albeit outside of marriage, while Nan's life is missing both a physical and a soul union that would make her happy. Conchita, it seems, has found a happiness that works for her (427). This is not the idealized union in love for either Nan or Wharton. Instead, it is a happiness based on material needs and satisfaction of physical desires.

Nan St. George, who has watched all the previous unions, is, perhaps, in the best situation to make an ideal match of soul and body. Her love relationships are the central interest of the novel and are presented in more detail than others. Nan is also the only character who rejects an unhappy physical relationship for a perfect union of soul and body while alive. It is the fact that Wharton actually plotted a happy ideal love match for her that makes her such a unique character in Wharton's fiction. Although Nan cannot experience her ideal union to its fullest until she suffers a pseudo-physical love and death touches her, the elements of death are not as prominent in this story as they have been in earlier novels. In fact, there really is not room for death relating to love in this new world. Even Nan's governess is too occupied with life to be concerned with "dead love affairs" (195). The women are too busy to have dead, idealized loves sidetrack them.

With Laura as the guiding force in Nan's upbringing, it is not unexpected that Nan will reject a dead love for the passion of the soul (195).

Early in the novel, Wharton categorizes Nan as being ruled by "waves of the blood, hot rushes of enthusiasm, icy chills of embarrassment and self-depreciation" (130). Her character makes her susceptible to outside influences and dreams. That dreams become key is obvious in her reaction to Jinny's lack of interest in Nan's dreams at Allfriars. Once her sister tells her to keep quiet about her dreams, "an iron gate seemed to clang shut in her; the gate that was so often slammed by careless hands" (239). Nan lives in her dreams and anyone who does not acknowledge and appreciate it sentences her to a lonely prison. Only a like mind that acknowledges and shares her dreams can set her free. Yet, despite Jinny's distaste at hearing Nan's dreams, Nan's early friendships are with romantic dreamers like Conchita and Laura. When the governess first arrives, the boys singing, "Nita, Juanita, ask thy soul if we must part" (163) greet her. Her answer shows that she knows about spiritual love. By inducting Nan into the world of Dante Gabriel Rossetti's more physical works, she demonstrates that she also knows about physical love. Even the fact that Nan is not as pretty as her sister and must wear Jinny's old clothes serves to drive Nan further into a dream world where she is a romantic beauty. Nan, at this point in her life, is still optimistic about love. She can imagine a love that lasts through the ages as easily as a fleeting love in her youth.

Nan's dreams also extend to the land around her. She sees beauty in houses that others think are prisons (239). Even Lady Churt's rented house takes on the incarnation of "a fairy galleon" to her (275). Yet, even this setting cannot improve the Duke. On his first visit to the American girls, he does not leave an imprint on any of them (281). When he finds Nan again outside of Runnymede, she cannot remember who he is and actually believes he is Mr. Robinson. In spite of that, however, the Duke surrounds himself with romantic images. His name, Tintagel, links him to the birthplace of King Arthur, the subject of many romantic stories and poems. They even meet in the ruined castle, which stirs Nan's imagination (283). The fact that her imagination is awakened to the fairy tales of her dreams accounts for her marrying the Duke. It is not the man that she marries, but the fantasy of Tintagel. Given that "the thought of visiting the scenes celebrated in Tennyson's famous poems had swept away all other fantasies" for her, one can imagine the impact that marrying the dream would have on her (286). It is impossible for her to imagine anyone who lived in that setting to be blind to the beauties of the land, the history and the literature. These are the beauties she thinks she is marrying when she marries the Duke. However, she refuses to "admit...[that] the ruins of the ancient Tintagel had played a large part in her wooing;...the idea of living in that magic castle by the sad western sea had secretly tinged her vision of the castle's owner" (369). To admit that, would be to admit that her imagination and dreams had misled her into a disastrous relationship.

The Duke even knows that she does not see the reality of his situation. When she sees him in the ruined castle, he is aware that her eyes reflect "not himself, but the sea" (299). His inability to see himself in her eyes plays into his dreams. The Duke, tired of being pursued by women (293), is looking for a woman with no knowledge of rank and titles (290). This innocence is exactly what he finds in Nan. It is important to note that he does not love her. As Laura finally realizes, he wants to marry Nan in order not to marry someone else (347–348). This alternative reality is exactly what the Duke envisions in Nan and expects from her. He marries the dream of what he thinks she is because it is his duty to marry. His image of her allows him the ability to escape from his mother's scrutiny. He persists in the marriage in spite of Laura's telling him that Nan will not always be what she is at the time of the proposal. For Laura it is obvious that "Nan is one thing now, but may be another, quite different, thing in a year or two. Sensitive natures alter strangely after their first contact with life" (347). The Duke, however, still believes in his dream of the innocent child and believes he will be able keep her from living life (347). Although he means well, it is not what Nan desires.

Nan, in a way, is marrying the romance of the land as much as the Duke is marrying an escape. It is interesting that she does not see the fog that rolls in to warn her that the Duke is not a good mate for her. Other signs are evident that she is moving in the wrong direction. Conversations between her and the Duke are difficult. In fact, the Duke falls into silence shortly after their conversations begin (304). This silence, when compared to the silence Nan and Guy share later, is a silence of loss, not shared minds. There is no natural ease and camaraderie. When Nan and Guy are silent, it is to see each other in the landscape and, therefore, to promote a deeper union between them. When Nan and the Duke are silent, it is to retreat into their respective dream worlds, thus promoting an even greater distance between them.

Somehow, in spite of these warning signs, Nan becomes the Duchess of Tintagel. Within two years of their marriage, both the Duke and Nan realize they cannot have their dream with each other. Although the Duke still fights to hold on to the childlike version of Nan he created, she has a crisis of selfhood. She questions who the woman with the new name really is (360). The one thing she is certain of is that this woman is not, and never will be, her true self. She is a stranger to herself, sharing the same body, but being completely separate entities. Even though she is not familiar with the new Annabel, the old Annabel no longer exists either (361). It is just as Laura predicted when trying to discourage the Duke. Nan's sensitive nature has changed once life and death have touched it. Instead of the Duke protecting her or their shared experiences bringing them closer together, it has driven them further apart. The death of the two children whom Nan loves drives the Duke further into his dreams and her further into the reality of love and death. They are not heading toward each other, but are heading on distinctly divergent paths.

Nothing can unite the two because neither Eros nor a union of souls is the basis for their relationship. They do not even have the shared emotion that Jinny and Lizzie have in their loves. They do not even have a shared imagination to see beyond the real. The Duke still has no time for the poetry his wife loves (364), and she still loves the castle for its romantic connections, not the man. In fact, the Duke sees the castle as a drain on his wealth, not a romantic ideal (369). The only time there is a mention of the Duke actually loving Nan is when he thinks of her as the mother of his child (378). In reality, he thinks he loved her only when she was fulfilling her duty as a duchess in giving him an heir. He loves her only when she is doing her duty. Nan does not allow herself such delusions anymore and, finally, openly admits that she should never have married the Duke (413). The simple conclusion she finds to rectify the mistake, divorce, horrifies the Duke's family.

It is at this low point in her life that coming face-to-face with Conchita's loving too many men leaves Nan feeling deficient for not finding love with anyone (431). The house becomes a tomb that is unbearable to her, and she needs to escape out into the world to find her "stormy self, reckless and rebellious" self (437). It is while she is seeking herself again that she also rediscovers Guy Thwarte, her soul mate. Given the heavy, overly overt symbolism surrounding Nan's and Guy's relationship, one tends to wonder if

Wharton would have toned it down, if she had lived to revise the novel. In any case, her depiction of their relationship shows an idealized love found on earth and in an earthly paradise. Although Wharton does not detail their original meeting, their second meeting is at Honourslove by the Love River. Guy not only believes in the beauty of Honourslove, but he also believes in the honor of love (226). He will neither taint love nor his land by marrying a woman with a fortune instead of a woman he loves (229). He is aware that marrying on a purely physical or monetary basis will not be a way to honor love. He also thinks too highly of Nan to ask her to wait for him forever while he sets out to earn his fortune. Their brief initial meeting speaks volumes about their suitability for each other in both a love of souls and physical love. Much like Nan, Guy has been brought up on Rossetti's art and poetry. He is in tune with both a soul love and a physical love, and he knows not to settle. Although at this stage in his life others see him as an undesirable match for a single girl, he is not seeking his fortune to win a wife. Instead, he will use his fortune to save his house, Honourslove. He is, however, a physically desirable match since Conchita wanted him for one of her matches.

Upon entering the grounds of Guy's estate, Nan felt connected "with the soft mellow place, as though some secret thread of destiny attached her to it" (256). She instinctively knows that this is where she belongs and where her heart belongs. As if to prove that he is worthy of her love, she and Guy have similar thoughts and feelings regarding the beauty of the land. Although they also walk in silence, they feel completely comfortable in each other's company (256). They feel a bond with each other and with the land that is only found between soul mates and cannot be forged.

Their moment of ultimate union occurs over a discussion "about the *beyondness* of things" (257). Nan does not have to explain to him what she means by "beyondness." Although "there's no such word," he immediately understands her meaning (257). Instead, he knows that it describes a feeling that takes two people experiencing it beyond life (257). The mere understanding of the term and the feeling without an explanation shows that these two are soul mates. Their moment of complete union includes not only each other, but also the land since it is the land which allows for their union. They are able to silently look at the land, seeing each other in the beauty before them (258). This description resembles Nick and Susy's when they were at Como. However, Nan and Guy do not have the moon as their guide so their relationship has the promise of a stronger bond. When compared with Lily Bart's and Selden's search to go someplace beyond, Guy and Nan are significantly closer to happiness in that realm. For Lily and Selden, beyond was an ideal place that they needed each other to find through belief in faith in themselves and their love. Nan and Guy have subtly modified the Republic of the Spirit to include the concept of "beyondness of things." This subtle, but significant, addition to the Republic extends the notion of beyond that Lily and Selden shared. Not only do Nan and Guy believe in a love beyond, but they realize that they can experience this love on earth through sharing the feeling of beyondness. It is mostly a feeling brought about by internalizing the beauty of place and people. This feeling, when with a soul mate, can be found in a place like Honourslove, where the occupants, although selling their treasures for the upkeep, honor love. This progression from the death-ridden, doomed romance in the life of Lily Bart and Selden to the understanding and potentially happy romance in life of Nan and Guy shows how far Wharton has come in her conception of love and romance with a soul mate. Yet, their achieving happiness is not easy. Wharton still cannot allow them to acknowledge the depth of their love until death has touched them both.

Before he left for South America, Guy thought that Nan was "the finest instrument…from which, when the time came, he might draw unearthly music" (393). Yet, that feeling ended when he learned she had married the Duke. He did not want to taint his dream of her with the fact of her marriage (393). She was the woman he aspired to love and, in part, she was part of the reason he worked so hard to amass his fortune. He finds it devastating that the Duke has won his prized soul mate. Guy knows that the Duke is wrong for her and will cause her harm. Once he learns of her marriage, he banishes her from his mind in a type of symbolic death. The once clear image of her eventually started to dull in his thoughts, she becomes more like a ghost to him (393). Her figurative death not only allows him to find love with Paquita, but also nearly allows him to fall victim to a "passionate impulse" not to return to England (389). However, he does not give in because the land means so much more to him.

After their first moment of communion, Nan and Guy are separated and seem to forget each other as they go on to lead separate lives. She enters her disastrous marriage to the Duke, and Guy marries Paquita. Guy's return to England is not as joyous as it should be since it is overshadowed by

Paquita's death. Interestingly enough, the deaths that effect both Nan and Guy are deaths of people the reader never sees; therefore, they are less sentimental deaths. There is less investment for the reader in these deaths than in previous works, which lessens the impact. Although Guy's loss seems to touch him more deeply than Nan's does, it never reaches the level of involvement the reader feels for the deaths of characters like Lily Bart and Bessy Westmore. The deaths do have an effect on Nan and Guy, however. He returns to Honourslove knowing that all the Thwarte "graves belonged to him, all were linked...in an old community of land and blood; together for all time, and kept warm by each other's nearness" (388). Paquita's death brings about an even greater appreciation and awareness regarding the connection among love, life, death and the land.

With Guy's return to England, the Correggio pictures of lovers surrounding Nan are no longer enough of an escape (404). Although the paintings are not mentioned by name, Wharton most likely had Correggio's paintings of mythological subjects in mind. Not only do these pictures exude physical sensuality, they also have elements of spiritual ecstasy. In essence, they depict the union of body and soul that Nan and Guy are seeking. Their spiritual union is still intact and rekindled when they are together. He understands her appreciation for the pictures and her distaste for doing things as the Dowager had without her having to tell him. When things go wrong, he is the one person she wishes to confide in and the one in whom she knows there would be complete understanding. Knowing he is around allows her to see the failure of her life with the Duke and have the strength to take the steps to rectify the situation. She finally realizes that her meeting the Duke "in ruin and a fog" at Tintagel symbolized the turn their life would take (428). She now believes that "lovers ought to meet under limpid skies and branches dripping with sunlight, like the nymphs and heroes of Correggio" (428). They ought to meet in the same way and setting she and Guy had met and established their union.

When she next meets up with Guy, it is in a sylvan "octagonal temple of Love" (437). Although the lords of Longlands had left the temple in ruins and full of abandoned game equipment, both Nan and Guy seek refuge there to think (437). For the Lords, the temple is a neglected place full of useless games, but for Nan and Guy, the place has an old, romantic beauty. The temple may be ruined, but the love still exists. This meeting is truly the beginning of their admitting their love for each other. As with other idealized love scenes in Wharton's works, the lovers meet high above the rest of the world in an insolated spot where others do not appreciate the beauty. Yet, their meeting is colored by emotions and feelings neither expected. Nan, who usually felt friendly comfort whenever Guy was near, feels angry with him (439). Her irritation shocks him since he had always "felt between them the existence of a mysterious understanding" (439). It appears as if the bond was broken. However, the more time they spend together in the temple, the closer they become and they renew the understanding between them. Guy finally admits to himself his physical desire for Nan, along with rekindling his spiritual desire for her. Although he wants to "comfort her with kisses," he knows she is not at the same place as he is quite yet (441). He is willing to suppress his desires in order to make her happy. In fact, their ability to understand each other allows him to believe that he would destroy their friendship if he tried to kiss her (441). He is willing to wait for Nan to develop an equal physical love for him. There are signs that she will reach the same physical love that he has reached because Laura and Conchita tutored her in the ways of passion and she does allow Guy to hold her hand.

Upon learning she would see Guy at dinner, Nan finally becomes concerned with her looks. She is aware that she does not wear the most beautiful dresses and that her hair should be styled differently. The poor duchess who had let the Dowager dictate her clothes finally makes her maid do her hair twice to look pretty to Guy, to appeal to his instincts of sexual selection. When he sees her, he notices "the change in her appearance, and the warm animation of her voice" (460). Her beauty shines through because she is happier at having him by her side.

When they visit Honourslove again, Nan first sees a ghost of her true self; she sees the woman she was before her name was linked with Tintagel. She is coming alive in the aura of Guy's balanced love. When she worries that her prison may outlast her, turning her into the suicidal Clärchen, Guy is there to tell her that he will show her all that there is to experience in life (466). Clärchen's song, found in act 3 scene 2 of Goethe's *Egmont*, is sung by a lover who contemplates suicide rather than be with someone else when she cannot save the man she loves. She would rather be dead than live a life without her true mate. Guy is there to show Nan that there is more to love than a suicidal ending, to continue her education in love. He does not want her to save him, but wants to continue their education together. He is unwilling to abandon her to a Clärchen-like ending. Although he will not protect her from the world, he will continue her education into it.

Knowing this allows Nan to relive the dream of an ideal romantic notion of love as a union of spirit and body. Her heart saw that

> in this great lonely desert of life stretching out before her she had a friend—a friend who understood not only all she said, but everything she could not say. At the end of the long road…she saw him standing, waiting for her, watching for her through the night. (470)

She is not the woman sitting alone in eternity waiting for the footstep which will never come. She is not alone. She has found a spiritual and physical love in life to give her a complete happiness and security that no other character in Wharton's works has experienced.

Although the text of their relationship ends here, Wharton's plot summary shows that she intended them to live a happy life together. Laura sacrifices her own love for Sir Helmsley for the pair so that she can see "love, deep and abiding love, triumph" over the barriers in its path (478). Finally, Nan and Guy have found each other and their true ideal love. As we have seen, allowing her characters to experience such a complete union of soul love and physical love is new for Wharton. Perhaps, she has finally come to the belief that one can find one's soul mate on earth. Eros no longer needs a more powerful Thanatos in order to find love. Instead, Eros is allowed to dominate Thanatos when one finds one's soul mate. Wharton has finally resolved the conflict between the two instincts. Both Eros and Thanatos work to create a union. At this point Wharton is able to see love and death as forces that "*affirm* a world of love and pleasure" (Brown 46). No longer does Wharton see love as a soul waiting for another soul, but as souls discovering each other, understanding and loving each other with a balanced love of body and soul.

CHAPTER ELEVEN

Conclusion

Love. It may be an old-fashioned notion in a thoroughly modern and postmodern world, but in the late Nineteenth and early Twentieth centuries it was also a concept in transition. With the influx of scientific theories regulating female sexuality, love and sex were entering a whole new realm. Through these changes love and the concept of love were undergoing a major redefinition. Scientists were not alone in their inquiries, as other writers were also examining the meaning of love in the modern world. Given the transitional nature of the concept of love, it should not be surprising that authors' theories of love were in transition also. Wharton was perhaps an unexpected person to enter into the discussion to the extent that she did. The scientific theories and philosophies which she studied did influence her developing concept of love. Eros and Thanatos appear in conflict throughout most of her writings, reflecting the tension between a physical (science based) love and a soul (philosophy based) love. In order to discuss the implications and conflicts between these two types of loves, Wharton created two Republics which were complementary and which were also in conflict. Her Republic of the Spirit, first vocalized by Selden in *The House of Mirth*, is a realm of the idealized transcendent love between like souls. This love is a romantic love of soul mates found in a realm beyond the physical, beyond earth, beyond the individual. It is a love of one soul for another, its mate, in an ideal realm based upon Plato's ideal of the separation of soul and body. Often, it is a character's imagination that leads the way to this love when the characters are above the world, secluded from the influence of outside forces. Characters who believe in this type of love also believe in a shared, unspoken language that binds their souls.

Although Wharton was a romantic and wanted to believe in the concept of love of souls, she was also aware of the factual evidence regarding love.

She knew, perhaps from experiences as much as from her reading Darwin, that more often than not physical urges were the source and inspiration of a lot of love matches. To accommodate this fact, Wharton envisioned a complementary Republic to complement and contrast the Republic of the Spirit. This faux Republic is a physical approximation of the other Republic. Characters in Wharton's works can use the faux Republic in different ways. Lily Bart, for example, tries to use the faux Republic to show Selden a signpost into the Republic of the Spirit. Bessy Westmore, however, prefers to live in the faux Republic because her imagination has not been trained to contemplate things of the rarer air of soul love. In later works, the faux Republic becomes a place of light and life.

Although only one Republic dominates a character's ideal view of love for the majority of Wharton's works, many of her characters strive to find a balanced love. They seek not only to balance the love of the soul with the love of the body, but in doing so they also seek to balance Eros and Thanatos. As Wharton moved away from believing in the idealized notion of love between soul mates, the enveloping aura of death slowly fades from her works. The early works are the ones with the strongest death imagery because, although some of the characters believe that they want a balanced love, they believe in the primacy of the love of the souls. As the primacy of physical love takes over, the strong death imagery begins to fade.

From the time she wrote "The Fullness of Life" to the time she wrote *The Buccaneers*, her view of love fluctuated between the primacy of the soul and the primacy of the body. Any attempt to draw a straight line of progression between the primacy of the soul to the primacy of the body would not be doing justice to Wharton's thinking. Instead, she saw at different times in her life a need for both types of love to take precedence. The more she learned about love and life, the more she felt that one needed a balance between the body and soul. Works such as "The Fullness of Life," *The House of Mirth*, *The Fruit of the Tree* and *Ethan Frome* have the strongest elements of death. In general, and to varying degrees, these are the ones in which the love of soul mates is seen as the ideal. These are the works in which the men involved are the ones who create the image of the ideal woman to which the real woman cannot or will not become, for it is thought to become so would be to lose herself and her identity. The men try to write the story for the women in their lives and the only way that can be fully accomplished is through the death of the woman involved. With the woman dead, she cannot change and, therefore, cannot ruin his idealized love for his romanticized creation.

Works such as *The Reef* and *Twilight Sleep* are equally distressing, but not for the death imagery, but for their conclusions. Anna Leath confronts both types of love, but cannot find happiness in either. Although she knows she needs to learn about both to find a balanced love, she ends the novel believing that she is the only one who believed in the love of the soul. Nona Manford in *Twilight Sleep* suffers a somewhat more cynical fate. She is surrounded by people who believe in one type of love to an excess, but cannot find a balanced view of love to emulate. Instead of believing in any form of love, she ends with having no belief in love at all.

Summer and *The Glimpses of the Moon* are two of the happier works in Wharton's fiction. Charity's life is at her happiest when she is awakened to Harney's physical love. There is even hope that she will find a balanced love with Royall at the end of the novel. Although Nick and Susy start out their lives as equals in the Republic, their physical needs pull them away from their bliss. It is only upon regaining status as equals that they can reenter a new, but slightly different, love for each other. Despite their flaws, they are happiest when they are able to love each other as equals.

It is somewhat comforting to know that Wharton's career ended with the depiction of love found in *The Buccaneers*. In this novel, she shows that there is more to love than just spiritual love and just physical love and, more importantly, that soul mates can find each other while on earth and live happily. Wharton is willing to entertain different notions of love; however, she still finds that it is impossible to build a lasting happy union on purely physical love. Instead, shared sympathies, ambitions, and understanding are the building blocks for a relationship. The ultimate love, however, is reserved for the ones who can see "the beyondness of things" (*Buccaneers* 257).

Bibliography

Works by Edith Wharton

Wharton, Edith. *A Backward Glance*. New York: Charles Scribner's Sons, 1964.
_____. *The Buccaneers*. Ed. Viola Hopkins Winner. Charlottesville: U P of Virginia, 1993. p. 119–483.
_____. *Ethan Frome*. New York: Macmillan Publishing Company, 1987.
_____. *The Fruit of the Tree*. Bridgewater, NJ: Replica Books, 1997.
_____. "The Fullness of Life." *Collected Short Stores of Edith Wharton*. Ed. Richard W. B. Lewis. Vol 1. New York: Macmillan Publishing Company, 1968. 12–20.
_____. *The Glimpses of the Moon*. Scribner Paperback Fiction, 1996.
_____. *The House of Mirth*. Norton Critical Edition. Ed. Elizabeth Ammons. New York: W. W. Norton & Company, 1990.
_____. *The Reef*. New York: Scribner Paperback Fiction, 1996.
_____. *Summer*. New York: Signet Classic, 1993.
_____. *Twilight Sleep*. New York: Scribner Paperback Fiction, 1997.

Works by Others

Ackerman, Diane. *A Natural History of Love*. New York: Vintage Books, 1995.
Allen, Brooke. "The Accomplishment of Edith Wharton." *The New Criterion* (September 2001): 33–40.
Ammons, Elizabeth. "Fairy-Tale Love and *The Reef*." *American Literature* 47.4 (Jan., 1976): 615–628.
Auchincloss, Louis. *Edith Wharton: A Woman in Her Time*. New York: Viking Press, 1971.
Barreca, Regina. "Introduction: Coming and Going in Victorian Literature." *Sex and Death in Victorian Literature*. Ed. Regina Barreca. London: Macmillan Press Ltd., 1990. 1–8.

Bassein, Beth Ann. *Women and Death: Linkages in Western Thought and Literature*. Westport, Conn.: Greenwood Press, 1984.

Bell, Millicent. Ed. *The Cambridge Companion to Edith Wharton*. New York: Cambridge UP, 1995.

Bender, Bert. *The Descent of Love: Darwin and the Theory of Sexual Selection in American Fiction, 1871–1926*. Philadelphia: U Pennsylvania P, 1996.

Benstock, Shari. *No Gifts from Chance: A Biography of Edith Wharton*. New York: Charles Scribner's Sons, 1994.

Bentley, Nancy. *The Ethnography of Manners: Hawthorne, James, Wharton*. New York: Cambridge UP, 1995.

Berry, Andrew, Ed. *Infinite Tropics: An Alfred Russel Wallace Anthology*. New York: Verso, 2002.

Bronfen, Elisabeth. *Over her Dead Body: Death, Femininity and the Aesthetic*. New York: Routledge, 1992.

_____. "Dialogue with the Dead: The Deceased Beloved as Muse." *Sex and Death in Victorian Literature*. Ed. Regina Barreca. London: Macmillan Press Ltd., 1990. 241–259.

Brown, Norman O. *Life Against Death: The Psychoanalytical Meaning of History*. Second ed. Hanover, NH: Wesleyan UP, 1985.

Colquitt, Clare. "Succumbing to the 'Literary Style': Arrested Desire in *The House of Mirth*." *Women's Studies* 20 (1991): 153–162.

Craig, Theresa. Edith Wharton: A House Full of Rooms, Architecture, Interiors, and Gardens. New York: Monacelli Press, 1996.

Darwin, Charles. *The Descent of Man, and Selection in Relation to Sex*. Princeton: Princeton UP, 1981.

De Rougemont, Dennis. *Love in the Western World*. Princeton: Princeton UP, 1940.

Dimock, Wai-chee. "Debasing Exchange: Edith Wharton's *The House of Mirth*." *Edith Wharton*. Ed. Harold Bloom. New York: Chelsea House Publishers, 1986. 123–137.

Du Plessis, Rachel Blau. *Writing Beyond the Ending*. Bloomington: Indiana UP, 1985.

Dwight, Eleanor. "Wharton and Art." *A Historical Guide to Edith Wharton*. Ed. Carol J. Singley. New York: Oxford UP, 2003. 181–210.

_____. *Edith Wharton: An Extraordinary Life*. New York: Harry Abrams, 1994.

Dyman, Jenni. *Lurking Feminism: The Ghost Stories of Edith Wharton*. New York: Peter Lang Publishers, 1996.

Elbert, Monika M. "Bourgeois Sexuality and the Gothic Plot in Wharton and Hawthorne." *Hawthorne and Women*. Ed. John L. Idol, Jr. and Melinda M. Ponder. Amherst: U of Massachusetts P., 1999. 258–270.

Erlich, Gloria C. *The Sexual Education of Edith Wharton*. Berkeley: U of California P, 1992.

Fedorko, Kathy A. *Gender and the Gothic in the Fiction of Edith Wharton*. Tuscaloosa: U of Alabama P, 1995.

Freud, Sigmund. *Beyond the Pleasure Principle*. New York: W. W. Norton & Company, 1961.

_____. *Civilization and Its Discontents*. New York: W. W. Norton & Company, 1961.

Fryer, Judith. "Reading *Mrs. Lloyd*." *Edith Wharton: New Critical Essays*. Ed. Alfred Bendixen and Annette Zilversmit. New York: Garland Publishing, 1992.

Gargano, James W. "*The House of Mirth*: Social Futility and Faith." *American Literature*. 44.1 (Mar., 1972), 137–142.

Gerard, Bonnie Lynn. "From Tea to Chloral: Raising the Dead Lily Bart." *Twentieth Century Literature* 44.4 (Winter 1998): 409–427.

Gerten-Jackson, Carol. "Correggio." *CGFA-A Virtual Art Museum*. http://cgfa.sunsite.dk/correggi.

Goodman, Susan. *Edith Wharton's Inner Circle*. Austin: U of Texas P, 1994.

_____. *Edith Wharton's Women: Friends and Rivals*. Hanover: U P of New England, 1990.

Grant. Michael. *Myths of the Greeks and Romans*. New York: Meridian, 1995.

Hoeller, Hildegard. *Edith Wharton's Dialogue with Realism and Sentimental Fiction*. Gainsville: UP of Florida, 2000.

Honey, Maureen. "Erotic Visual Tropes in the Fiction of Edith Wharton." *A Forward Glance: New Essays on Edith Wharton*. Ed. Clare Colquitt, Susan Goodman and Candace Waid. Newark: U of Delaware P, 1999. 76–99.

Holbrook, David. *Edith Wharton and the Unsatisfactory Man*. New York: Vision Press, 1991.

Hutchinson, Stuart. "Sex, Race, and Class in Edith Wharton." *Texas Studies in Literature and Language* 42.4 (Winter 2000): 431–444.

Joslin, Katherine. *Edith Wharton*. New York: St. Martin's Press, Inc, 1996.

_____. "Architectonic or Episodic? Gender and *The Fruit of the Tree*." *A Forward Glance: New Essays on Edith Wharton*. Ed. Clare Colquitt, Susan Goodman and Candace Waid. Newark: U of Delaware P, 1999. 62–75.

Kassanoff, Jennie A. "Extinction, Taxidermy, Tableaus Vivantes: Staging Race and Class in *The House of Mirth*." *PMLA* 115.1 (2000): 60–74.

Kaye, Richard. *The Flirt's Tragedy: Desire Without End in Victorian and Edwardian Fiction*. Charlottesville, VA.: UP of Virginia, 2002.

Killoran, Helen. *Edith Wharton: Art and Allusion*. Tuscaloosa: U Alabama P, 1996.

Lacan, Jacques, *Ecrits: A Selection*. Trans. Alan Sheridan. New York: W. W. Norton & Company, 1977.

Levine, Jessica. *Delicate Pursuit: Discretion in Henry James and Edith Wharton*. New York: Routledge, 2002.

Lewis, R.W.B. *Edith Wharton: A Biography*. New York: Fromm International, 1985.

Lewis, R.W.B. and Nancy Lewis. Eds. *The Letters of Edith Wharton*. New York: Collier Books, 1988.

Louis, Margot K. "Proserpine and Pessimism: Goddesses of Death, Life, and Language from Swinburne to Wharton." *Modern Philology*. 96.3 (Feb. 1999): 312–346.

Loeffelholz, Mary. *Experimental Lives: Women & Literature 1900–1945*. New York: Twayne Publishers, 1992.

Loving, Jerome. "The Death of Romance: The Portrait of a Lady in the Age of Lily Bart." *A Forward Glance: New Essays on Edith Wharton*. Ed. Clare Colquitt, Susan Goodman and Candace Waid. Newark: U of Delaware P, 1999. 100–115.

Michelson, Bruce. "Edith Wharton's House Divided." *Studies in American Fiction*. 12.2 (Autumn, 1984): 199–215.

Miller Budick, Emily. *Engendering Romance: Women Writers and the Hawthorne Tradition, 1850–1990*. New Haven: Yale UP, 1994.

Miller Hadley, Kathy. *In the Interstices of the Tale: Edith Wharton's Narrative Strategies*. New York: Peter Lang Publishers, 1993.

Milton, John. *Paradise Lost. The Riverside Milton*. Ed. Roy Flannagan. New York: Houghton Mifflin Company, 1998. 296–710.
Montgomery, Maureen E. *Displaying Women: Spectacles of Leisure in Edith Wharton's New York*. New York: Routledge, 1998.
Nettels, Elsa. *Language and Gender in American Fiction: Howells, James, Wharton and Cather*. Charlottesville: UP of Virginia, 1997.
Olin-Ammentorp, Julie. "Edith Wharton, Margaret Aubyn, and the Women Novelist." *Women's Studies* 20 (1991): 133–139.
Ovid. *Metamorphoses*. Trans. Rolfe Humphries. Bloomington: Indiana UP, 1983.
Papke, Mary E. *Verging on the Abyss: The Social Fiction of Kate Chopin and Edith Wharton*. New York: Greenwood Press, 1990.
Penny, Nicholas. Ed. *Reynolds*. Weidenfeld, London: Royal Academy of Arts, 1986.
Pfeiffer, Kathleen. "*Summer* and Its Critics' Discomfort." *Women's Studies* 20 (1991): 141–152.
Plato. *Phaedrus*. Trans. W.C. Helmbold and W.G. Rabinowitz. New York: Macmillan Publishers, 1956.
_____. *Symposium*. Trans. Robin Waterfield. New York: Oxford UP, 1998.
Preston, Claire. *Edith Wharton's Social Register*. New York: St. Martin's Press, 2000.
Ramsden, George. *Edith Wharton's Library*. Settrington, Stone Trough Books, 1999.
Scholl, Sharon. *Death and the Humanities*. London: Bucknell UP, 1984.
Schriber, Mary Suzanne. "Convention in the Fiction of Edith Wharton." *Studies in American Fiction* 11.2 (1983): 189–201.
Showalter, Elaine. "The Death of the Lady (Novelist): Wharton's *House of Mirth*." *Edith Wharton*. Ed. Harold Bloom. New York: Chelsea House Publishers, 1986. 139–154.
Singley, Carol J. *Edith Wharton: Matters of Mind and Spirit*. Cambridge: Cambridge UP, 1995.
Springer, Marlene. *Ethan Frome: A Nightmare of Need*. New York: Twayne, 1993.
Stange, Margit. *Personal Property: Wives, White Slaves, and the Market in Women*. Baltimore: Johns Hopkins UP, 1998.
Stevenson, Pascha Antrece. "Ethan Frome and Charity Royall: Edith Wharton's Noble Savages." *Women's Studies* 32 (2003): 411–429.

Vita-Finzi, Penelope. *Edith Wharton and the Art of Fiction*. London: Pinter Publishers, 1990.

Wagner-Martin, Linda. *The Age of Innocence: A Novel of Ironic Nostalgia*. New York: Twayne Publishers, 1996.

Waid, Candace. *Edith Wharton's Letters from the Underworld: Fictions of Women and Writing*. Chapel Hill: U of North Carolina P, 1991.

Walker, Barbara G. *The Women's Encyclopedia of Myths and Secrets.* New Jersey: Castle Books, 1996. 669–673.

Waterfield, Robin. Introduction. *Symposium*. By Plato. New York: Oxford UP, 1998. xi–xl.

Wershoven, Carol. *The Female Intruder in the Novels of Edith Wharton*. East Brunswick, New Jersey: Associated University Press, 1982.

White, Barbara A. *Edith Wharton: A Study of the Short Fiction*. New York: Twayne Publishers, 1991.

Wolff, Cynthia Griffin. *A Feast of Word*s*: The Triumph of Edith Wharton*. New York: Addison-Wesley Publishing Company, 1995.

———. "Lily Bart and the Beautiful Death." *American Literature* 46.1(Mar.1974):16–40.

Index

Adam, 36, 37, 54, 86
Adam Tempted, 36
Amherst, John, 45–63, 70, 77, 125
Andromeda, 34, 39, 40

Bart, Lily, 2, 3, 23, 24, 25, 26, 27, 28, 29, 30, 31, 32, 33, 34, 35, 36, 37, 38, 39, 40, 41, 42, 43, 45, 46, 47, 52, 54, 57, 58, 62, 63, 71, 80, 101, 125, 131, 144, 145, 150
Beauty, 4, 5, 8, 9, 14, 17, 24, 27, 31, 32, 34, 35, 36, 39, 40, 41, 46, 47, 48, 50, 51, 55, 56, 57, 59, 60, 69, 81, 83, 87, 89, 91, 97, 98, 111, 127, 128, 129, 136, 137, 140, 144, 145, 146
Berenson, Bernard, 6
Beyond, 3, 9, 10, 11, 15, 18, 19, 21, 22, 23, 24, 25, 26, 27, 28, 30, 32, 33, 34, 35, 38, 39, 41, 42, 45, 48, 50, 53, 55, 56, 57, 58, 61, 69, 83, 84, 86, 88, 89, 91, 96, 100, 102, 107, 110, 112, 118, 119, 120, 127, 130, 131, 137, 142, 144, 149
Beyondness, 9, 135, 143, 144, 151
Body, 3, 4, 6, 8, 9, 17, 19, 36, 42, 46, 52, 54, 55, 59, 60, 67, 68, 69, 70, 72, 73, 74, 75, 76, 77, 81, 85, 88, 93, 94, 99, 106, 110, 115, 118, 119, 123, 127, 128, 131, 132, 133, 139, 142, 145, 147, 149, 150

Brent, Justine, 45, 46, 47, 48, 50, 51, 52, 53, 54, 55, 56, 57, 58, 59, 60, 61, 62, 63, 70, 77, 100, 126
Buccaneers, The, 9, 10, 11, 87, 89, 101, 133, 135–48, 150, 151

Communion, 17, 18, 25, 26, 29, 30, 31, 32, 33, 39, 41, 42, 43, 57, 61, 63, 71, 72, 76, 89, 90, 115, 144
Correggio, 145

Dance, 69, 72
Darrow, George, 11, 80, 81, 82, 83, 84, 85, 86, 87, 88, 89, 90, 91, 92, 93, 94, 99, 102, 116
Darwin, Charles, 1, 3, 4, 5, 13, 14, 16, 26, 27, 35, 36, 43, 45, 46, 66, 70, 79, 80, 96, 127, 128, 150
Death, 1–11, 13, 14, 15, 19, 20–25, 26, 28, 30, 31, 33, 34, 37, 38, 39, 40, 41, 42, 43, 45, 46, 47, 49, 52, 53, 55, 56–61, 65, 66, 67, 68, 69, 71, 72, 73, 74, 75, 76, 77, 79, 86, 87, 91, 92, 94, 95, 98, 104, 105, 106, 107, 112, 115, 116, 117, 120, 124, 126, 130, 132, 135, 139, 142, 144, 145, 150, 151
Desire, 4, 6, 7, 8, 13, 14, 19, 22, 25, 26, 27, 29, 33, 34, 35, 38, 39, 47, 48, 49, 50, 51, 55, 63, 65, 70, 72–76, 78, 79, 80, 81,

82, 84, 85, 90, 92, 93, 97, 100, 101, 104, 107, 108, 109, 116, 125, 127, 136, 146
Dorset, Bertha, 24, 25, 26, 29, 46

Eros, 1, 3, 4, 6, 7, 8, 10, 14, 17, 20, 22, 23, 27, 28, 29, 30, 34, 37, 39, 41, 106, 142, 147, 149, 150
Ethan Frome, 10, 11, 52, 63, 65–78, 79, 85, 95, 100, 150
Eve, 54, 86

Faith, 22, 25, 42, 55, 59, 60, 61, 90, 107, 114, 116, 117, 118, 120, 121, 123, 131, 133, 144
Freud, Sigmund, 1, 5, 6, 7
Friendship, 25, 45, 53, 84, 101, 107, 108, 109, 127, 141, 147
Frome, Ethan, 10, 11, 52, 65, 66, 67, 68, 69, 70, 71, 72, 73, 74, 75, 76, 77, 78, 85, 95, 101, 126
Frome, Zeena, 66, 67, 68, 69, 70, 72, 73, 74, 75, 76, 77, 126
Fruit of the Tree, The, 10, 43, 45–63, 67, 77, 86, 100, 125, 150
Fullerton, Morton, 2, 14
"Fullness of Life, The", 5, 10, 13–22, 23, 28, 32, 49, 92, 100, 150

Glimpses of the Moon, The, 11, 91, 107–21, 151
Grave, 42, 76, 98, 102, 120, 132
Gryce, Percy, 24, 25, 29, 30, 80
Harney, Lucius, 95, 96, 97, 98, 99, 100, 101, 102, 103, 104, 105, 106, 151
Heuston, Stanley, 123, 124, 125, 126, 127

House of Mirth, The, 10, 43, 23–43, 49, 52, 54, 57, 80, 83, 135, 149, 150

Ideal, 1, 3, 4, 5, 8–11, 14, 16–28, 30, 33, 35, 36, 37, 38, 40, 41, 43, 45, 47–52, 55, 57, 58, 59, 61, 62, 65, 66, 70, 71, 75, 76, 80, 85, 89, 93, 96, 97, 98, 100, 104, 106, 108, 109, 110, 113, 114, 116, 117, 118, 120, 124, 125, 129, 130, 136, 139, 142, 144, 147, 149, 150
Imagination, 25, 26, 30, 33, 35, 36, 37, 38, 47, 48, 50, 53, 55, 61, 74, 80, 81, 83, 84, 85, 87, 88, 89, 94, 98, 107, 112, 119, 136, 140, 141, 142, 149, 150

Lacan, Jacques, 6, 7
Language, 5, 6, 17, 21, 56, 65, 66, 76, 88, 96, 99, 101, 104, 149
Lansing, Nick, 107, 108, 109, 110, 111, 112, 113, 114, 115, 116, 117, 118, 119, 120, 121, 123, 143, 151
Lansing, Susy, 107, 108, 109, 110, 111, 112, 113, 114, 115, 116, 117, 118, 119, 120, 121, 123, 143, 151
Lapsley, Gaillard, 95
"Last Giustiniani, The", 3
Leath, Anna, 11, 78, 79, 80, 81, 82, 83, 84, 85, 86, 87, 88, 89, 90, 91, 92, 93, 94, 102, 151

Manford, Nona, 123, 124, 125, 126, 127, 128, 129, 130, 131, 132, 133, 151

Index

Manford, Pauline, 53, 126, 129, 130, 131, 132, 133
Marriage, 1, 2, 8, 9, 14, 15, 21, 36, 46, 49, 50, 51, 52, 53, 55, 56, 58, 60, 61, 66, 67, 70, 73, 80, 83, 85, 89, 98, 102, 104, 105, 107, 108, 109, 110, 111, 112, 113, 117, 118, 119, 120, 123, 126, 128, 129, 136, 137, 138, 139, 141, 142, 144
Milton, John, 54, 86
Mivart, St. George, 16, 17
Moon, 109, 110, 113, 116, 117, 121, 143
Mrs. Lloyd, 36, 37

Norton, Sarah, 3

Ovid, 39

Pale, 33, 34, 37, 46, 58, 74, 77, 90, 91, 98, 111, 116
Paradise Lost, 54
Passion, 2, 9, 18, 20, 41, 49, 56, 65, 67, 70, 79, 80, 81, 82, 83, 86, 87, 89, 92, 93, 94, 95, 101, 125, 127, 129, 138, 146
Perseus, 34, 39
Phaedrus, 3, 4, 45, 47, 53, 81
Philosophy, 1, 2, 3, 7, 9, 46, 53, 112, 149
Physical love, 13, 14, 15, 16, 17, 18, 20–28, 30, 31, 32, 33, 39, 41, 43, 45–52, 54, 55, 56, 57, 59, 60, 61, 62, 63, 65, 67, 69, 70, 71, 76, 77, 78, 79, 80, 81, 82, 84, 85, 86, 87, 88, 89, 90, 91, 94, 95, 98, 99, 100–110, 116, 117, 119, 120–130, 132, 135, 137, 138, 139, 140, 143, 145, 146, 147, 149, 150, 151
Plato, 1, 3, 4, 5, 14, 17, 20, 22, 24, 26, 27, 43, 45, 46, 47, 53, 81, 103, 126, 149

Reef, The, 11, 78, 79, 94, 79–94, 99, 100, 106, 116, 151
Republic of the Spirit, 10, 22, 25, 27, 31–36, 38, 39, 40, 41, 42, 43, 45, 48, 50, 51, 52, 53, 54, 55, 57, 58, 70, 71, 72, 76, 83, 86, 88, 89, 96, 98, 99, 100, 101, 104, 107, 108, 109, 110, 111, 112, 113, 114, 119, 121, 131, 144, 149, 150, 151
Reynolds, Sir Joshua, 36, 37
Romantic, 1, 2, 3, 4, 5, 10, 16, 20, 23, 25, 30, 32, 34, 36, 37, 38, 39, 45, 46, 56, 66, 69, 71, 75, 76, 80, 82, 85, 89, 90, 93, 94, 95, 106, 108, 109, 110, 112, 120, 123, 124, 129, 130, 132, 135, 138, 139, 140, 141, 142, 144, 145, 147, 149
Royall, Charity, 94, 95, 96, 97, 98, 99, 100, 101, 102, 103, 104, 105, 106, 116, 151

Sacrifice, 21, 30, 47, 62, 111, 113, 125, 126, 132, 137
Science, 1, 2, 3, 7, 9, 130, 149
Selden, Lawrence, 23, 24, 25, 26, 27, 28, 29, 30, 31, 32, 33, 34, 35, 36, 37, 38, 39, 40, 41, 42, 43, 45, 46, 47, 52, 53, 57, 71, 83, 101, 131, 144, 149, 150
Sex, 5, 7, 8, 149
Sexual selection, 1, 4, 5, 13, 16, 27, 35, 45, 46, 50, 66, 79, 80,

81, 89, 97, 101, 124, 128, 136, 138, 146
Silence, 65, 66, 67, 70, 76, 84, 85, 101, 127, 141, 143
Silver, Mattie, 65, 66, 67, 69, 70, 71, 72, 73, 74, 75, 76, 77, 78, 85, 101, 104
Sled, 52, 58, 73
Song, 66, 96, 103, 146
Soul mate, 1, 2, 9, 10, 16, 17, 19, 20, 21, 22, 25, 28, 29, 30, 33, 34, 36, 48, 50, 53, 59, 60, 63, 65, 70, 71, 74, 81, 82, 84, 85, 87, 89, 90, 92, 94, 96, 101, 108, 110, 115, 116, 117, 118, 123, 124, 127, 142, 143, 144, 147, 149, 150, 151
Spiritual love, 1, 3, 4, 9, 10, 11, 13–19, 21, 22, 23, 24, 25, 26, 27, 29, 30, 31, 33, 35, 37, 38, 39, 41, 42, 43, 45–52, 54, 55, 59, 60, 61, 63, 65, 69, 71, 73, 76–83, 85, 86, 88, 89, 91–96, 98, 103, 104, 105, 106, 107, 108, 109, 110, 117, 118, 120, 121, 123–127, 130, 132, 135, 137, 138, 139, 140, 143, 144, 145, 146, 147, 149, 150, 151
St. George, Annabel, 9, 87, 101, 135, 137, 138, 139, 140, 141, 142, 143, 144, 145, 146, 147
Summer, 11, 79, 91, 94, 106, 95–106, 151
Symposium, 3, 4, 14, 45, 81, 103

Thanatos, 1, 3, 6, 7, 10, 23, 28, 37, 147, 149, 150
Thwarte, Guy, 87, 101, 135, 141, 142, 143, 144, 145, 146, 147

Twilight Sleep, 11, 53, 123, 130, 123–34, 151

Union, 1, 4, 9, 10, 11, 14, 15, 16, 17, 18, 19, 20, 22–33, 35, 38, 39, 42, 43, 46, 48, 49, 50, 51, 54, 56, 57, 59, 60, 61, 62, 63, 76, 79, 80, 82, 85, 86, 89, 93, 98, 99, 103, 108, 110, 123, 124, 125, 126, 127, 130, 132, 133, 135, 137, 138, 139, 141, 142, 143, 145, 147, 151

Valley of Decision, The, 10
Vampire, 28, 39, 65, 74, 76
Veil, 46, 53
Viner, Sophy, 11, 79, 80, 81, 82, 83, 84, 85, 86, 87, 89, 90, 91, 92, 93, 94, 99, 102, 104
Voice, 13, 15, 19, 35, 53, 66, 67, 77, 85, 96, 97, 103, 104, 105, 124, 146

Wallace, Alfred Russel, 16
Westmore, Bessy, 46, 47, 48, 49, 50, 51, 52, 53, 54, 55, 56, 57, 58, 59, 60, 61, 62, 63, 67, 77, 125, 145, 150
Wharton, Edith, 1–6, 9, 10, 11, 13, 14, 15, 17, 19, 20–23, 27, 28, 29, 43, 45, 46, 48, 50, 56, 63, 65, 66, 70, 71, 73, 76, 78, 79, 84, 85, 86, 87, 88, 90, 93, 94, 95, 98, 100, 101, 103, 105, 106, 107, 108, 109, 110, 111, 118, 120, 121, 123, 124, 126, 127, 130, 133, 135, 136, 137, 139, 140–147, 149, 150, 151
Wharton, Teddy, 14

MODERN AMERICAN LITERATURE
New Approaches

Yoshinobu Hakutani, *General Editor*

The books in this series deal with many of the major writers known as American realists, modernists, and post-modernists from 1880 to the present. This category of writers will also include less known ethnic and minority writers, a majority of whom are African American, some are Native American, Mexican American, Japanese American, Chinese American, and others. The series might also include studies on well-known contemporary writers, such as James Dickey, Allen Ginsberg, Gary Snyder, John Barth, John Updike, and Joyce Carol Oates. In general, the series will reflect new critical approaches such as deconstructionism, new historicism, psychoanalytical criticism, gender criticism/feminism, and cultural criticism.

For additional information about this series or for the submission of manuscripts, please contact:

> Peter Lang Publishing
> P.O. Box 1246
> Bel Air, MD 21014-1246

To order other books in this series, please contact our Customer Service Department at:

> 800-770-LANG (within the U.S.)
> (212) 647-7706 (outside the U.S.)
> (212) 647-7707 FAX

Or browse online by series at:

> www.peterlang.com